CW01558912

THE HISTORY OF THE DEVIL

THE HORNED GOD OF THE WEST

BY

R. LOWE THOMPSON, B.A.

Author of " The Hunter in Our Midst"

LONDON

KEGAN PAUL, TRENCH, TRUBNER & CO., LTD.

BROADWAY HOUSE: 68-74 CARTER LANE, E.C.

1929

Kessinger Publishing's Rare Reprints
Thousands of Scarce and Hard-to-Find Books!

- .
- .
- .
- .
- .
- .
- .
- .
- .
- .
- .
- .
- .
- .
- .
- .
- .
- .
- .

We kindly invite you to view our extensive catalog list at:
http://www.kessinger.net

PLATE I

THE MAGICIAN OF THE OLD STONE AGE.

A masked man wearing the horns of a stag and a horse's tail, drawn at least 9,000 years ago in the Caverne des Trois Frères. Ariège, France. Magdalenian Culture. (After a photograph by Count Bégouen. From Sollas, *Ancient Hunters.* Macmillan & Co.)

PRINTED IN GREAT BRITAIN BY
BILLING AND SONS, LTD., GUILDFORD AND ESHER

TO

NINA TOYE

CONTENTS

CONTENTS

CHAPTER V

WITCH GOD AND DEVIL

CHAPTER VI

THE EVOLVED MAGICIAN

CHAPTER VII

HERNE AND HIS KIN

CHAPTER VIII

THE DECLINE OF THE DEVIL

CHAPTER IX

MAGIC TO-DAY

LIST OF ILLUSTRATIONS

PLATES

IN THE TEXT

PREFACE

SINCE this small work is itself little more than a preface, or introduction, to a very wide field of inquiry, I believe that I may best serve the reader here by mentioning a few works of a readable nature wherein he will find further information and illustrations, that I have had to omit, together with references to more technical publications. Here, also, I would express my indebtedness to the authors of these works and to others whom I have acknowledged in the text; though I must at the same time remain responsible for the use which I have made of their observations and for the line of country that I have taken.

First, then, anyone who wishes to look up his remote ancestors may consult Prof. G. G. MacCurdy's *Human Origins* for a general survey of Europe; Prof. W. J. Sollas' *Ancient Hunters* which contains, amongst many others, an illustration of the Lourdes Magician, to which I have referred; Prof. H. Obermaier's *Fossil Man in Spain*, which also has excellent illustrations; and the numerous plates in Mr. M. C. Burkitt's *Prehistory*. These works—should the reader's faith in archæology have been shaken by the recent frauds at Glozel—will establish the authenticity of the remains upon which I have based the early part of my thesis. In some cases, however, I have modified the statements of these authors as to the age of the remains and the cultures to which they belong in view of later findings that have, for the most part, been clearly set forth by Mr. Harold Peake (whom I must also thank for having called my attention to the valuable article on harlequin in *The Quarterly Review*) and Dr. H. J. Fleure in their recent work, *Hunters and Artists*. Modern parallels to ancient beliefs will be found in numerous collections, such as Sir James Frazer's *Golden Bough*, though this has grown into a mighty forest in which a hurried reader is somewhat apt to get lost. Amongst the few men who can feel with living savages or " think black," and also convey to others some idea of the savages' mentality—which is very different to that usually ascribed to them by those who dwell in libraries—I would mention the names of Mr. Kidd, who wrote *The Essential Kaffir* and Dr. Malinowski. In regard to the Gallo-Roman and Celtic beliefs, the literature is so vast and usually of such a specialized nature, that I am reluctant to send any reader who asks for bread to the usual quarries that are so largely composed of stones. Figures, however, of the Horned God, Cernunnos, accompany an article by A. Bertrand on " L'Autel de Saintes et les Triades Gauloises " in the *Revue Archæologique* for 1880. For the witch cult we have two contrary views: that taken by Miss M. Murray in *The Witch-cult of Western Europe—An Anthropological Study*, and the very Catholic and medieval view adopted by the Rev. M. Summers in his *History of*

PREFACE

Witchcraft and Demonology and *Geography of Witch-craft*, both of which have extensive bibliographies. Dr. Carus also touches upon this phase in his *History of the Devil*, although that work is more especially concerned with the metaphysical aspects of the concept of evil.

The survival of these ancient beliefs to-day and of the mental processes that lie behind them, and the fact that concepts once useful to man may in the course of time become highly injurious to his welfare: these are points which I must leave the reader to discover for himself. That is, if this short sketch is to be anything more than a solace for some curious hour.

For the preparation of the blocks and for permission to reproduce the illustrations that I have used, I am indebted to the generosity of the following authors and publishers:

Dr. Carus, *History of the Devil*, Open Court Publishing Co., Chicago, for Figs. 3, 4, 5, and 6.

Prof. G. G. MacCurdy, *Human Origins*, Appleton and Co., for Plates II., IV., V., and Fig. 1.

Prof. W. J. Sollas, *Ancient Hunters*, Macmillan and Co., for Plates I., III., and Fig. 2.

Rev. M. Summers, *History of Witchcraft and Demon-ology*, Kegan Paul, Trench, Trubner and Co., for Plates VI. and VII.

Plate VIII. is reproduced by permission from the Sir Benjamin Stone collection of photographs in the Birmingham Reference Library.

PREFACE

And now in the time-honoured phrase let me " cut the cackle and come to 'osses," cave-bears and bison, aurochs and reindeer on which men lived when the devil was once a god.

R. LOWE THOMPSON.

January, 1929.

THE HISTORY OF THE DEVIL

CHAPTER I

THE BELIEF OF THE STONE AGE MEN

The oldest shrine in the world—The thought of a savage—Palliatives for death—The mental vitamine—The feast as a social bond—The idea of luck—The magic art of the caves.

IT may seem a far cry from the figure of a magician painted by Stone Age men 9,000 years ago to that of the harlequin who still appears in pantomime; the connection between a Celtic deity and an English folk dance may seem to be obscure, and yet these are the relationships which I wish to trace. Using this sequence as a thread, I shall endeavour to bring out some of the vital factors which led to the persistence of a most primitive cult, and I shall also try to string upon my thread some current superstitions. The poet Donne has written in one of his songs:

"Go and catch a falling star,
  Get with child a mandrake root,
Tell me where all past years are,
  Or who cleft the devil's foot."

And while I regret that I cannot comply with Donne's conditions, I hope at least to solve the last problem which he propounds.

B

THE HISTORY OF THE DEVIL

The facts which I use mainly refer to Western Europe, where the prehistoric material has been most closely studied and where the belief in question, being relatively free from the complexities which we find in the cults of the ancient East, can be more clearly seen. But though the sequence from a pre-Roman deity to a medieval cult and to vestigial remnants at the present day is unbroken, there is admittedly a gap in the prehistoric record between the magicians of the Old Stone Age and the occurrence of a horned god in the early Iron Age. This gap, in my opinion, is due to the lack of material evidence, to 'the imperfection of the prehistoric record,' rather than any real lack of continuity. The fact that the cult endured in historic times, in spite of the most dire persecution, testifies to its vigour, and it must have been even more vigorous and deeply engrained when such magic was still an integral part of the life and thought of primitive men. To support my opinion, however, I must discuss the origin and essence of such magic and mention some of the similar practices which exist all the world over amongst living savages. As in embryology and comparative anatomy, only a general treatment can make the sequence clear, and only a realization of the practical value of magic, the 'survival value' to the human organism, can explain the persistence and the power of old beliefs.

It is always advisable to push back an inquiry as far as possible, so I begin at the close of the last inter-glacial period, which, according to the short system of dating that I shall adopt for the sake of clarity, may be placed

somewhere around 35000 B.C. We then find Old Stone
Age weapons which are so crude that they represent what
is known as the 'Pre- or Proto-Mousterian' culture that
precedes and almost certainly evolved into the full
Mousterian culture, which is definitely associated with
that most distinct species of fossil man, *Homo
neanderthalensis*. Writers are perhaps too apt to picture
Neanderthal Man as a ferocious and irreligious animal,
but even in the more rudimentary pre-Mousterian culture
we must modify this view owing to some curious remains
from the three Swiss caves at Côtencher, Wildkirchli, and
Drachenloch. Of the first two caves I will only say that
the bones of the cave-bear constitute from 95 to 99 per
cent. of all the animal remains that are found in the pre-
Mousterian deposits. The real interest lies in the
Drachenloch, for here in the corresponding layers we have
a hearth, a kind of platform of flat stones, and the oldest
altar in the world, which was piled up with skulls of the
cave-bear. A special kind of tool was made from the shin
bone of the same animal, and these tools were found " by
hundreds at Drachenloch, as many as twenty-five or thirty
having been found in a single heap." The lofty position
of this cave—it is 8,028 feet above sea level—recalls the
remote sacred caves which we shall meet with in France
and Spain, and it certainly seems that we have here a
record of the most ancient animal cult that has been discovered.

During the Fourth and last glacial period this culture
gave way to the Mousterian culture. There is no direct

evidence of an animal cult, though bear meat was still popular, the remains of over 800 bears having been found in one cave alone; but we do find in some cave burials a respect for the dead, which is surprising in such an uncouth animal as Neanderthal Man. Thus, a boy at Le Moustier had been buried with an axe and a scraper next to his hand and seventy-four other artifacts; his skull rested on a pillow of crushed flints, and a large auroch bone lay above it. A man at La Chapelle-aux-Saintes, who lay with his feet towards the west, had also been buried with a large number of tools and some lumps of yellow ochre; the leg bones of a bison lay over his skull, and as one of these was still in connection with the smaller bones of the foot, it was probably covered with a meat offering for the deceased. Two trenches near by contained masses of ash and bone. A similar trench of 'funeral baked meats' was found in the family vault at La Ferrassie, where the six skeletons also lay from east to west. The heads of two of these had been covered by stone slabs. The Neanderthals then, like our own poor, buried their folks 'with ham' or at least beef, and the grave goods may be taken as an indication of some belief in survival after death, in a happy hunting ground where weapons would be necessary and ochre would clothe an eminent person with respectability. *Mutatis mutandis* it would be the well-furnished heaven that still appeals to many men at the present day.

Now I have not introduced the customs of Neanderthal men as the starting-point for my genealogy of the devil.

That will begin later, when the first representatives of that other species *Homo sapiens* (a term which also includes all the races of men who are alive to-day) entered Europe shortly after the last great glaciation had reached its second maximum, and conditions were beginning to improve. The probability that these newcomers took over any beliefs from the Neanderthals is remote. We have no evidence that the two species ever interbred; their crafts are quite dissimilar, and the disappearance of the aboriginal species does not suggest any friendly intercourse or peaceful penetration. The resemblances, therefore, which occur between these early practices and later cults, which also centre round a food animal or a dead body, can best be regarded as examples of convergence and as the expressions of certain fundamental modes of thought (or rather feeling) and lines of action that will arise independently in any hunting community. As a background to the later and more definite cults, we may take some suggestions concerning the origin of these simple practices.

In the first place, we have a very primitive people who lived entirely by hunting and collecting, and in Central Europe showed a marked preference for the flesh of the cave-bear. They have a cult of the cave-bear, and to find out the underlying motives we must try to feel with them. We must detach our minds from the more reasonable and scientific modes of civilized thought. We must pass from our orderly system of cause and effect into a crazy world largely governed by caprice, where the dividing lines that we set between our waking life and our dream life, or between man and beast, are blurred and indistinct; where a man's spirit may leave his body and wander in distant fields; where beasts may seem to speak with a human voice. The critical faculty which begets reason, the vainglory which leads us to believe that we act mainly by reason, the pride which makes man deepen the gulf between himself and other animals; all these are late developments in our evolution. Thus the savage thinks more by analogy and on the principle of *post hoc ergo propter hoc:* whence comes the strength of magic and much medicine. In dreams or visions or trances the spirit of a savage has strange adventures in strange lands, and yet his body has remained in the same place; thus he comes to believe in the existence of a 'soul' which can leave his body. In dreams, also, he may see the forms of those long dead, of his parents or some impressive person in a malignant or a benignant guise. What then is simpler or more natural than to feel and imagine that they still exist in some unknown sphere? Moreover, this belief in survival after death will comfort him in the rare moments when he reflects, with horror, upon the problem of death and is confronted by the facts of decomposition. Like the anonymous hero in *The Hunting of the Snark*, the possibility that he will " softly and suddenly vanish away " is to the savage "a notion I cannot endure." A dim belief, then, in a happy hunting ground—without too great an insistence on the possibility of a less pleasing alternative— will help to keep up his spirits in times of adversity, and by strengthening his 'Will to Live' and powers of endurance, will come to have a real survival value. Again, owing to the possibility that malignant ghosts, who can certainly make him wake in a cold sweat of terror, may injure him in other ways, it becomes advisable to treat the dead bodies of eminent personages and their relatives with respect.

By analogy we have the animistic beliefs which likewise endow beasts and trees, and even stones and streams and storms, with some kind of spirit similar to that of the hunter. Linked with this, there is the idea that some kind of essence or 'virtue' resides in the beast. A group of hunters feels the obvious benefit when it has killed and devoured a large animal. What, then, is more natural than the supposition that men may, at the same time, absorb and benefit by the spiritual essence of the beast? The critical faculty is undeveloped; no hard and fast lines are drawn—why, indeed, worry to do so—between physical and psychical nutrition: and, all the world over, people will eat the flesh of courageous animals to gain courage and avoid the flesh of timorous beasts, lest they become infected by their cowardice. By a very natural progression specific virtues may become associated with different parts of an animal's body: when, for example, one English boy will tell another that if he eats fishes' eyes he will be able to see under water; or the grease of a shaggy bear has a vogue as a hair restorer.

Again, when a savage believes that a human ghost can injure him, he may have a strong misgiving that the ghost of such a formidable beast as a bear may also make itself unpleasant. This idea would seem to lie behind customs like those of the Ainu bear hunters, who, after they have killed their favourite beast in a firm but most apologetic manner, set up the skulls in a place of honour and offer libations to them from time to time. The sacred, or at least the favoured, animal is both reverenced and eaten. But now, since I do not wish to attribute too much to the Neanderthals, I will pass from the individual aspect to the simplest social aspect of such cults.

Amongst the various factors which have led to man's pre-eminence, few are more important than those which tend to strengthen his gregarious impulses and bind together a group of men into a more effective social unit. In early days, and especially during a glaciation, the family hearth would be a most effective focus, and round it a huddled group could develop their language and a corporate sense. Next to fire there is, perhaps, in man's leisure hours, no material bond that is more powerful than the social meal. From a beanfeast to a banquet, from a health to the highest sacrament, men can best realize and reinforce group-feeling by this means. To simple minds this method is most successful when there is food galore; and this would be the case when a large beast was slain, and the fierce spirit of the bear—a nine foot cave-bear was a true *pièce de résistance*—would render the orgy more impressive. That meat would have been hard won, an outward and visible sign of prowess, like mayoral turtles or other rare and exotic luxuries which linger both on the tongues and in the minds of later men of 'taste.' The bear feasts in the caves and the funeral feasts would, there-fore, serve as a valuable bond; and when man's body is satisfied crude fancies may run free. The communicants might come to regard themselves as the Brotherhood of the Bear—we have still our Bear patrols, not to mention the Ancient Order of the Buffaloes—later they might have a blurred idea of kinship with the bear or descent from a super-bear, like the Saxon eorl Siward, 'Son of the Fairy Bear.' They might absorb its spirit not only by eating its flesh, but by wearing its teeth as amulets or its skin as a busby . . . but I anticipate.

The only points that I wish to dwell upon at this early stage are the remote origins of some belief in our survival after death; the endowment of animals with a similar spirit; the advisability of propitiating such spirits; and the early occurrence of the sacramental feast. I must also note the pragmatic value of such beliefs, however absurd they may seem in alien or heterodox cultures, and that this value lies in the extra confidence which they give to the individual and in the development of a corporate spirit and a new *morale* throughout the group. I may add that these values are the more important at a time when the instinctive impulses, which will give a cornered rat the courage of despair or the purer instincts which make a young rabbit 'freeze' or enable an ant community to function as a perfect whole, are being laboriously replaced by more intelligent behaviour. It is a case of new lamps for old, and while men were yet in this state of transition from hereditary impulses to acquired modes of action, they would need all the support that they could derive from such vague spiritual fare.

The simple cults, which I have described, arose, I believe, independently amongst the various races of both *Homo neanderthalensis* and *Homo sapiens* in response to the primary needs of the simple hunter. In any case they will serve as the dim background from which more definite rites have sprung.

At a provisional date of about 14000 B.C. there is a real break in the history of Europe, for the first known representatives of *Homo sapiens* crossed from North Africa into Italy and into Spain. Since I am not here concerned with the racial types which anthropologists have tried to establish from the scanty skeletal remains, I will simply use cultural terms and speak of the Aurignacians and Magdalenians who occupied France, Central Europe, and the northern coast of Spain from about 14000 B.C. to 7000 B.C.; and the Capsians, with a distinct culture which was dominant in North Africa and the greater part of Spain throughout this period.

The general view of these cultures is that the Aurignacian peoples (one of which has been popularized as the 'Cro-Magnon Race') evolved under congenial conditions till about 11000 B.C., when a steppe folk from Asia, with what is called the Solutrean culture, invaded the European grasslands and occupied them for a thousand years or so, after which they seem to have retreated and were replaced by the Magdalenians. From the continuity of the art, the Magdalenian culture probably developed from that of the Aurignacians who had survived in the hills and in the West. Towards the close of this period there was a return to colder conditions; the reindeer reappeared in France (the Magdalenians are sometimes spoken of as the 'Reindeer Men'); and the culture, which extended into Russia and probably across northern Asia, was modified. But in spite of this cold, their art then reached its zenith, fostered, perhaps, rather than repressed by a greater need for endurance and by longer periods of inactivity. The Solutreans, with open camps, left little behind them but their distinctive weapons, and may be regarded as a passing episode. The Aurignacians and Magdalenians used caves, and in these we have the marvellous remains that reveal the early beliefs of man in a more definite form.

Let us take the Aurignacians. The cave burials, which I imagine were those of important people, amply testify to their reverence for the dead. If we glance at those near Mentone we find amongst the grave goods many tools, crowns and breastplates of shells, pillows of stone and bone, elaborate necklaces of bone and shell, and lumps of pigment. Many of the bones were reddened with ochre, a curious practice which was prevalent during this latter part of the palæolithic age. There are also carved pendants made not only from bone and shell, but from less familiar objects, like fossil coral, greenstone, the diseased growth in a mammoth's tusk, and human teeth. Man, through his persistent desire to heighten his bodily consciousness, to show off, to gain good luck, or to ward off evil influences, now uses charms and attaches rarity values to objects that have no intrinsic worth, but like our mascots, talismans, and amulets, inspire him with a sense of power and protection. Such charms may definitely derive their virtue from the fact that they have once formed a part of some revered animal or man; at a second remove because they have once been in contact with such a being; and at a third remove—a natural root or a flint formed like a bear or like a cross—because they bear some resemblance to or suggest the sacred object. Or again—and this is a very primitive point which I might have mentioned before—the attention of a savage, like that of a magpie or a child, may be attracted to any bright or unusual object; and, treasuring it as his very own, he may come to regard it as a vehicle for that less definite idea of luck which anthropologists call 'mana.' Such an action is based on a belief that some kind of unspecialized luck or virtue is loose in the world and may be tapped by certain objects or by certain actions. This belief in mana in its indefinite and vague form can best be realized if we think how, as children or as adults, we may have picked up some stone or other object and have come to regard it as lucky. Any gambling crowd is apt to be ridden by lucky numbers, days, acts, or objects which may be the recognized symbols of some lost or living cult, or again may be credited with supernatural powers simply because they have appealed in some vague way to the individual. Such beliefs save us— as all men wish to be saved—from the haunting fear that we are bound as helpless forms upon the wheel of fortune.

Turning to the animal cults we have an astounding mass of evidence since these Aurignacians and Magdalenians were inspired artists. Their remote ancestors had doubtless noticed the spoor of animals and scratches we still can see in the cave walls where the bears had sharpened their talons. Like children, they had doubtless filled in idle hours by scrabbling with sticks or by imprinting their hands, as a sign manual, upon wet mud; they would whittle sticks and cut bone, or mess about with lumps of plastic clay. From such beginnings their cave art evolved in an unbroken sequence. We have simple, incised outlines of animals showing only two legs; then better profiles showing four legs, and by additional scratches the eyes and hoofs and fringes of shaggy hair. The incised lines were often filled in with red or black pigments, and in a local phase, the whole body might be coloured with a flat 'wash,' or rather daub. Lastly, we pass to the Magdalenian masterpieces in which the bodies of the animals, though still outlined with scratches, are delicately shaded in tones of brown and red and yellow. This art is essentially naturalistic and not conventional; the animals are most life-like; they were drawn by men who were soaked in the essence of the beasts, upon whom their lives depended. Many caves are filled with these pictures, but I will only mention two details: that an early (two-legged) Aurignacian elephant had been drawn with a large triangular patch to mark the position of its heart, and that spears are sticking into some of the Magdalenian horses and bison.

13

Now it is not enough to say that these hunters indulged in 'Art for Art's sake' from a purely æsthetic impulse. If the Bushmen, whose paintings have such a marked resemblance to this palæolithic work (but more particularly to the Capsian school), appear to do so at the present day, it is probably because in their degeneration the original motives have been lost. Again, though savages will elaborate designs upon their weapons, clothes, and personal effects out of sheer pleasure and self-esteem, these paintings were fixtures on the walls of the tribal cave. But we may dismiss the idea of a purely artistic motive when we consider that in the first place these men, with but few exceptions, only painted food animals; and in the second place had their finest art galleries in pitch dark and barely accessible caves.

Let me take the first point. If we place the subjects in their order of frequency we find that the wild horse easily heads the list (except in Spain, where the red deer is most popular), and then come numerous figures of red deer, bison, goats, wild cattle, reindeer (in a colder phase), and smaller deer, then less abundantly the mammoth, rhinoceros and bear, and more rarely still the boar, chamois, musk ox, seal, and elk. The hare, which plays such an important part in later superstitions, only appears twice; and for some obscure reason, unless we have confused it with the goat, the sheep only occurs once. Inedible animals are represented by some lions and wolves and an occasional hyena, glutton, fox, badger, and otter. Birds are not frequent, but here and there one can pick out a few swans, geese, ducks, a grouse, and an owl. Fish occur more commonly than birds, and can be doubtfully recognized as salmon, pike, and flatfish. There is one representation of a snake. In brief, the artists drew and carved little save the larger ungulates, whose bones are found around their hearths, and a few of the more dangerous carnivores. The smaller food animals which could be more easily captured hardly appear at all, and then do so as a rule upon portable objects which would have some peculiar significance. The vegetable kingdom is only represented by about six feeble designs on bone.

The second point can best be illustrated by a few of the most famous galleries. At Niaux the paintings are half a mile from the cave entrance; at Font-de-Gaume one must crawl for 130 yards through a dangerous passage; the discoverer of the virgin cave at Montespan had to crawl and swim for 1,300 yards along the channel of an underground stream; at Tuc d'Audobert the caverns can only be reached by tortuous routes, and here, as elsewhere, the most significant drawings are placed in the most remote chambers. These artists, with their small oil lamps or torches, were most retiring fellows. We can safely assume that these pictures were the outcome of a definite cult with rites which had a real bearing upon the life of the tribe; and an examination of three caves may help us towards some understanding of the practical (and as we would say, from our modern point of view, the mystical) motives which underlie this art.

The first caves are those of the Tuc d'Audobert, Ariège,

France. They were discovered by the Count Bégouen in July, 1912, and in the following October he noticed a chimney-like opening high up on the side of one of the galleries. This led to a narrow passage which, in the course of time, had almost been sealed up by stalagmite, but the Count cut his way through and came out into an antechamber. In the words of Prof. Sollas : " We linger awhile to admire its beauty. It is adorned in chastest splendour with white stalactite, which lines the walls, depends from the roof in myriads of pointed spears, threads the air in a maze of slender columns, and spreads upon the floor in a lacework of little basins filled with silent pools of water. We pass on, and soon enter the magician's chamber —chapel, workshop, what you will—and there, leaning against a mound in the middle, are the creatures of his art. Two bisons modelled to the life, one a bull . . . and the other a cow. Only one side is completely modelled, the other, which rests against the rock, is left in the rough." The work is 9,000 years old at least and yet quite modern. In the same hill lies the Caverne des Trois Frères, which contains a gallery of over 400 pictures, while at the far end, painted high up so that it dominates the entire chamber, is the picture called 'The Sorcerer,' or as I prefer to call it 'The Magician' (see Frontispiece).

The cavern of Montespan in the Pyrenees, with its awesome approach, was a cave which had been untrodden since the days of the Magdalenians. The walls were incised with animal forms, and beyond these were the clay models of a lioness, half a woman's body, some clay balls, and the remains of other models which had been spoilt by a drip of water from the cave roof. A kind of side chapel might have impressed our pre-Mousterians, for in its centre, on a sort of raised platform, there was the statue of a sitting bear. The head was missing, but a hole in the neck suggests that there might have been a peg on which a head could be fixed, and indeed the skull of a young bear of the right size lay between the paws. The whole floor of this chapel had once been covered with models, and all of them had been repeatedly jabbed with spears. This last point is important.

These caves, and many others, simply reek of the magic which I wish to analyze.

CHAPTER II

THE POWER OF MAGIC

How magic will arise—The magician of the Old Stone Age—The animal guise—Killing by effigy—The dancing faun—Birth rites and ancient rites.

BEFORE trying to interpret these models and paintings of animals and magicians, we must, in theory at least, try to see how a belief in magic arose in the first instance. I have already taken some suggestions as to the general origins of a belief in ghosts and souls and the practice of killing and eating sacred animals. This in turn leads to 'Contagious Magic,' where mere contact is sufficient to establish a mystic bond, and by a further analogy to the universal magic based on a 'Law of Similarity' whereby, for example, a cowry is taken as a fertility symbol, or a lung-like lichen is used as a remedy for pulmonary disease. Behind these there is also the vague idea of a circumambient and impersonal 'mana' which, however, since a savage prefers to think in terms of the concrete rather than the abstract, continually becomes attached to definite objects. So far such contagious and homeopathic magic has mainly been impressed upon man by external objects, but another form of homeopathic or imitative magic may also express the internal emotional states of a savage or of a savage group.

18

THE POWER OF MAGIC

Following Malinowski, we may take some individual reactions. Let us say that a hunter has no luck; he waits in vain for his prey; all his knowledge has failed him, and he feels helpless. The hours pass; his hopes and desires increase; he sees in his mind derisive beasts or a magnificent catch of fish. His patience is exhausted; his passions surge within him; he cannot remain inactive, and he breaks out into action, inviting the animals to 'come on' and brandishing his spear. It is the usual body-and-mind reaction, and his words and gestures will fit the end which he has in view. They will be imitative or mimetic. The reaction may be almost unconscious: when, for example, we think of a hated enemy and clench our fists, or a bored sailor whistles for the wind. These are familiar examples, and we must remember that a savage, in his foggy world, will react more strongly to his emotions, like a child who may confuse his world of 'make-believe' with dull reality. In an extreme form we can see this mimicry in many cases of mental derangement, hypnosis, and that peculiar malady, la-ta.

Now even a cat may gain some relief from her muscular and nervous tension when she twitches her tail and chatters her teeth at an elusive sparrow. Similarly, the hunter has relieved his mind, and, moreover, is often left with a sense of a satisfaction and an impression that his desire has been or will be fulfilled. The thing is 'as good as done.' By his pantomime he may feel that he has really blasted his enemy, or that the game will come along. He can settle down again with more composure and confidence. Therein lies one value of an oath.

But it may so happen that the game does appear; that his enemy does come to grief; that, if he has whistled long enough, the wind will rise. Then, since the critical faculty is, as I have said, a plant of slow and uncertain growth, the savage will not distinguish between causation and coincidence. Why should he, for he will be greatly pleased to think that *his* improvisations have attained their end? We are, indeed, only too familiar with the type of mind that still prefers a supernatural to a natural explanation of any strange phenomenon; that is thrilled and fortified by a sense of mystic power or divine favouritism; and is a living witness to the debt which humanity owes to the babies' 'comforters,' the swaddling clothes, and stays of magical beliefs.

There will, of course, be failures—the game may not arrive—but, and here is another foundation on which magic rests, the human mind is so constituted that one positive result outweighs a hundred failures. The prophecies about important events that have been fulfilled might be written in a small notebook; those that have not would fill a library. Yet any prophet can still find an audience. This mechanism is akin to that which banishes unhappy memories of pain and failure, which, were they not outweighed by pleasant thoughts, would hinder our chances of success. There are, of course, more obvious incidents which favour the growth of a belief in magic. It may happen that out of a bolus of remedies, selected because they look like a liver, one may have some purgative value; or bear's grease and *friction* may stimulate one's hair. Again, a man passing through a dark wood peopled by real and imaginary terrors will keep up his spirits and try to ward off evil by appropriate words and gestures. If he comes through unscathed he tells the tribe. If his prayers have not been effective against a marauding lion, he will have no tale to tell. We do not hear of the mascots that did not stop the bullet; nor does a fisher dwell upon the failure of some sure-killing charm. But given success, each budding magician will tell his tale; often with added detail. Then the transition from such spontaneous and individual magic to more stereotyped social beliefs is an easy one. Even our private oaths— when a golf ball becomes 'possessed'—develop a sameness and become trite. The wonder-tale becomes fixed by repetition round the hearth; children will learn it at their mother's knee. The salient points become impressed upon an audience of savages, who, like our dogs with their set ways and fancies, or our own children, are firm ritualists and will mislike any marked deviations from the standard form.

We must also reckon with spontaneous words and gestures which will arise when a group of hunters take the field together; when they give tongue as a herd, or mimic the gestures of a defiant leader. We have the stronger power of massed emotion, the contagion of crowd feeling. The endless chants of the Kaffirs as they run or row or clear their lands are often meaningless, but meaning may enter them and turn to magic. And deeper causes may call forth magic as an antidote to despair. Man, as a diurnal animal, is most open to attack at dusk, when, perhaps, he has not yet reached his shelter and his protecting fires, or his vitality is lowered after a long day's work. Thus E. P. Marais notes that just about sunset the wild baboons, which he studied, "became profoundly and causelessly depressed. They gathered in groups, assumed attitudes of profound dejection, and repeatedly uttered their cries of mourning even at times when things were going very well with them. . . . A careful inquiry revealed the fact that ten per cent. of the Europeans in our vicinity felt the same psychological melancholy. It passed as darkness set in. Among 'wild' Kaffirs it is almost universal." He adds that this 'Hesperian depression' is amply illustrated by such hymns as 'Abide with me; fast falls the eventide' and various melancholy nocturnes. Such a condition favours the growth of magic. A group will be impelled to yowl in chorus; or, better still, to sing more lustily. The deep-rooted emotions of a communal hunt will act in a like manner. In both cases time will be taken from a leader, and recognized chants and gestures will be adopted and become fixed. Lastly, such expressions of group feeling will be employed, not only at the actual moment of a crisis, but in anticipation and as a part of a definite routine in the hunters' life.

Returning to the caves, we can now see why the Aurignacian elephant had a heart, why some figures have spears in their flanks, and why the clay models had been jabbed.

THE POWER OF MAGIC

The hunters no longer express an overwhelming desire by stabbing visions in the air; they pretend to wound or actually disfigure representations of the beasts. I need hardly say that many living savages practise this magic, sometimes as an emergency measure, which helps them to endure, and often as a regular practice which will give them confidence before they set out to hunt or to make war. Amongst the Ojibwa Indians, the medicine-man thrusts at the red heart of a painted beast and chants repeatedly:

> " I shoot your heart; I hit your heart.
> Oh, animal . . . your heart . . . I hit your heart."

Many negro tribes also indulge in such repetitions, maybe for days, and they are hardly 'vain' when we consider the power of suggestion. These Stone Age hunters had their empirical Coué. Amongst primitive and emotional savages the importance of such rites can hardly be exaggerated. As Kidd rightly observes of the Kaffirs, " the natives fight with most marvellous bravery when they are assured by their doctors that success is certain; in fact, everything turns on the sense of impending victory, for the natives lose heart quickly in a forlorn hope." Confidence and a strong will to live on the patient's part win many a fight to-day for our modern doctors. Faith-healers also emphasize this point; though I do not know how they deal with that well-known symptom, *spes phthisica*, the radiant hope of so many consumptives just before they die.

When magic has crystallized out from such cloudy

origins, men will slowly, but very surely, employ any means by which their rites can be rendered more effective. They will try to create conditions which lay the mind open to suggestion. The caves, where a dim religious light turned to black darkness, lit only by feeble illuminants, would produce more than 'Hesperian depression.' After toiling in single file for half a mile underground the devotee would be in a fit frame of mind for any initiation or great sacrifice. A like mood may also be induced by sound or motion. For the hold of rhythm, from a cradle song to the beat of a drum, or a revivalist hymn, from a swinging gait to the Dionysiac frenzy of a religious dance, lies partly in its power to lull the conscious mind and to expose the unconscious mind to the suggestions of a leader and the transcendent emotions of the herd, till men become filled with exultation and capable of strange deeds. We have no evidence that these hunters had loud musical instruments, but some drawings do suggest a dance, and I have little doubt that they would chant in unison.

Generally speaking, also, the stranger the objects employed in magic the greater is their power. Unfamiliar costumes, weird charms, garbled sounds, the unseemly and dangerous ingredients of a witches' caldron, may excite the derision of the modern sceptic, but when men breathed magic like air and were more spiritual, their very power lay in their absurdity. The cave-man would not say, 'I believe because it is impossible,' but he would none the less feel and believe most fervently. Mystery still has its value. Our prescriptions are written in Latin; our menus are in French; and scientists still rejoice in hypertrophied terminologies.

But to sum up. It is from such dim origins and then amidst more definite rites that the magician will emerge. By directing the magic he will strengthen the hunter's arm and the social bond; he will guard a tribe against despair and a fatal lethargy; he can appease the spirits of a sacred animal or a dead chief. He derives his power from the essential mind of man; he serves the vital needs of his community; and as long as these needs remain the same—the maintenance of the food supply and the fertility of both man and beast—he will not greatly change. In this lies the vitality of the figure that now appears.

Representations of the human form very rarely occur in Aurignacian and Magdalenian art. In the earlier culture we have only one bas-relief of a man and about a dozen statuettes and a bas-relief of fat women, which, like the example shown on Plate III., all seem to have a symbolic meaning. In the Magdalenian phase, barely twenty figures have been found and, with the exception of one clay model, all, as far as one can see, are male figures that have a special significance. The reason why ordinary members of the tribe are not represented—they are in the contemporary Capsian art of Spain—is twofold. In the first place, the primary aim of these cults was to gain mastery over food animals. In the second place, it would be perfectly natural for these men to assume that if one could injure a food animal through its effigy, one could in the same way harm a human animal. Any attempt at portraiture would, therefore, be fraught with danger both to the subject and to the artist, who would be suspected of evil intent and sorcery. Here I am using the word 'sorcery' to denote the unauthorized and illicit practice of magic by an individual for his own ends; whereas true magic in its origin is an orthodox affair with rites and observances that are carried out for the good of the community as a whole. The distinction is an important one, because this cave magic must at present be regarded as an essential part of tribal life. Secret though the caves may be, they were used for the most holy, but not for illicit, cults, since we find that magic designs occur freely on the implements and utensils in everyday use. The magician, then, is a protector of society, and, if any rebels existed, one of his duties, like that of the recognized and official witch-doctors of the Zulus, would be to 'doctor,' or, in other words, root out, any 'witches' or unqualified practitioners. This possibility is indicated by the fact that even when human figures occur in the Capsian paintings their features are not drawn, the heads being mere ovals, so that an enemy wishing, let us say, to injure Smith, could not, if he defaced a picture, be certain that he was not by an oversight bringing calamity upon friend Jones. The only exceptions to this Capsian practice are certain plumed figures that are drawn on a larger scale than the ordinary hunters and warriors. These have sometimes pronounced features and may be generalized types, or more probably represent chiefs and their (slightly smaller) magicians, who might well be deemed immune to this mode of attack.

THE POWER OF MAGIC

Of the simple Magdalenian type we have three figures that are obviously men disguised in the heads and skins of chamois, and two of these are bounding with a vigour that betokens some inspiring rhythm (Fig. 1). These were carved on short implements that go by the name of

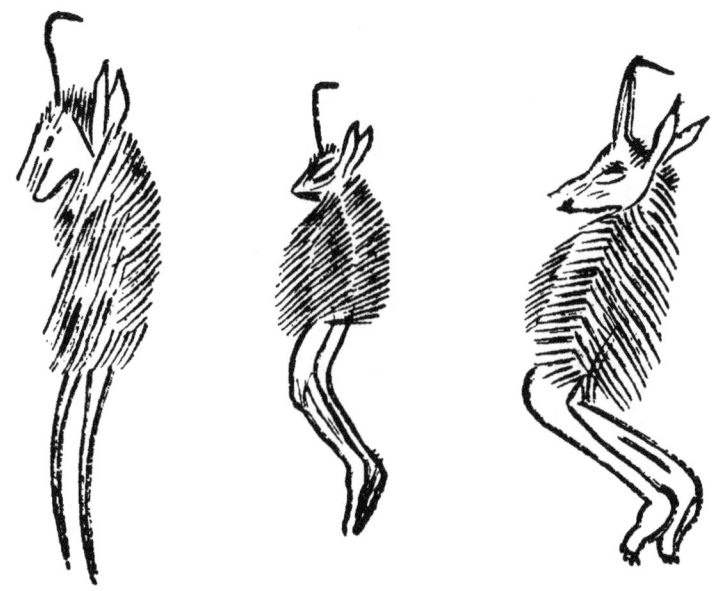

FIG. 1.—DANCERS IN CHAMOIS SKINS.

Three figures engraved on a bâton found in the rock shelter of Mège, Teyjat, Dordogne, France. Actual size. Magdalenian Culture, c. 10000-7000 B.C. (After Capitan and Breuil. From MacCurdy's *Human Origins*. Appleton and Co.)

'bâtons,' and are frequently found in Magdalenian deposits. They are usually pierced with round holes, and similar tools are still used by some Eskimos for smoothing down their fishing lines of hide and sinew and for straightening them out when they get snarled. Many of the bâtons, however, are so beautifully carved and engraved into the heads of animals or birds that they were doubtless

27

used as symbols of authority by chiefs or magicians, just as the mace becomes a sceptre or the shepherd's crook is converted into a crozier. Elsewhere, both in France and Spain, the Magdalenians have drawn figures that are dancing in a still more excited manner; and, though their bodies may be naked, their faces are certainly masked. The person shown on Plate II. has possibly utilized the head of a bear. Other examples figured by Obermaier and by Sollas also have certain points in common. Thus, four at Altamira in Spain all have lengthy muzzles; in the Cave of Marsoulas, Haute Garonne, three masks only are shown, two of which have very large noses and, with their bald pates, also bear a marked resemblance to a magician from Lourdes, that even then was a very holy place.

The cream of the collection, however, is the magician of the Caverne des Trois Frères, in the South of France (see Frontispiece). And here I will quote the impression given by Sollas: "It presents a remarkable combination of the horns of a stag, a face like an owl's, a long beard, the ears of a wolf, the tail of a horse, the paws of a bear, and the feet of a man. The body and thighs are striped, probably to represent the pelt of some animal. It seems to symbolize in one person fleetness, wisdom, penetrating vision, and strength. Whether these attributes were attributed to the wizard himself or to some mythical being it is impossible to say." Without wishing to subscribe to all these identifications, we can clearly see that we are dealing with a masked man who is wearing a stag's antlers and a horse's tail. The stripes, which are laid on in black pigment, may be inter-

28

PLATE II

A MASKED DANCER OF THE OLD STONE AGE.

An engraving on a rondelle of bone found in the Mas d'Azil, Ariège,
France. Magdalenian Culture, c. 10,000—7,000 B.C. (After Piette.
From MacCurdy, *Human Origins*. Appleton & Co.)

preted as the ceremonial paint that is used to enhance so many mysteries, rather than an actual pelt, which would surely have been indicated with greater skill. The question as to how far the identity of the magician became merged into the personality of a deity would hardly arise. A savage, especially when he is in the throes of a mystery, will not trouble himself about such speculations. The Greek talent for metaphysics had not yet troubled the world.

The Lourdes magician is a cruder engraving upon a piece of schist (like the one clear drawing of a hare), yet he has enough in common with the mural example to tell us that the cult has assumed a definite form with recognized vestments for its leader. He has, at least, the tail of the principal food animal; the long beard may show us that these hunters, like the Zulus, had a great respect for the wisdom of an ancient; and we may, I think, accept Sollas' idea that the divergent scratches above his head are meant for the horns of the second most important food animal. The mixedness of the two figures need not surprise us, for the caves also contain curious figures such as a lion with three heads (like Cerberus who guarded the gates of Hades), a bear with the head of a wolf, another with the tail of a bull, and so on.

In all these figures the salient point is the animal guise of the performer, the use of chamois skins, animal masks, or horns and tails; and in this we can see the apotheosis of an animal cult that I discussed in my preamble. To sum up a possible line of evolution, we can start with the most natural assumption that the psychical as well as the physical properties of an animal may be transferred by eating its flesh, by eating particular parts of the body in which particular qualities are supposed to reside, or by washing and rubbing oneself with the blood or such parts of the beast. Then men believe that they can gain the same results by wearing parts of the beast, in which case the virtues are transferred by contact rather than actual assimilation, and, lastly, by wearing representations of the beast. The two last advances would be more decorative, more economical, and more continuous in their action. They also depend upon and serve to illustrate the fundamental belief that a mystic bond continues to exist between the sacred animal and anything which has been in contact with, or is a representation of, that animal.

Nor does the matter stop here, for in the savage mind such an invisible bond will be like a road along which magic may pass both backwards and forwards. Conversely, then, we have the belief that animals or men may be influenced when magical rites are performed over some fragment of their anatomy, such as a nail paring or a lock of hair; over something that has been in contact with them, like a footprint or unconsumed portions of their food; and, finally, over an effigy, which, like a shadow, is regarded as an emanation, an extension, or, more simply, a 'part' of their personality. In virtue of such a bond, magic and medicine, like the impromptu and spontaneous actions of a distressed hunter, can operate at a distance. The performance will be of an imitative nature and will be accompanied by any accessories that will render it more impressive, such as a dim light, rhythmic chants and dances, rare and curious medicines, weird spells and incantations, which gain power by repetition, painful initiations, orgiastic festivals, and the like.

We can only guess at the nature of these palæolithic rites, but we can safely assume that the performers, after they had been tuned up to the right emotional pitch by various social forms of excitation and the personal ministrations of the magician, mutilated clay images to secure good hunting.

I shall generalize about the character of magicians later on, but we can here consider certain factors which may have determined their attire. We can note the primitive use of skins as clothing and their more definite use as a disguise in stalking animals; when Bushmen, for example, disguise themselves and imitate the movements of a buck or an ostrich so successfully that they can mix with and kill the beasts at a close range. Similarly, children love to play at being animals, and such play serves not only as a safety-valve, but as a practice which co-ordinates brain and muscles and enables them to break down 'instinctive' or impulsive modes of action and to replace them by skilled and acquired movements with artificial weapons. Such rehearsals by children or by adults must be essentially mimetic if they are to lead to success in the field. The actor must for the nonce 'be' the animal. He must, both literally and metaphorically, get into the skin of his part. These are material factors, and I would not, therefore, care to maintain that a magical motive lies behind all garments of fur or feathers *wherever* and *whenever* they are worn. It is natural that the hunting chief should be more or less disguised as a lordly beast, but, at the same time, we must suspect a magical motive where we find that such habiliments have a definite form (and a mixed form at that) and are used on special occasions and under peculiar conditions. Here there is no doubt that we have magicians, with the strong probability that the insignia of the sacred beasts conferred spiritual values upon the wearers. How far the magician, though he would be recognized as a human being in private life, was regarded as animalized or quasi-divine in his official capacity we cannot say, but it is well to bear in mind the ease with which a harmless masquerader may, in an infant's mind, suddenly assume a terrifying and unearthly aspect, and the persistent belief of living savages in the true metamorphosis of a human being into a werewolf or a witch-hare.

Such a rôle, not only as a leader in suggestion ritual, but as a man-animal or an animal-man, can develop on several lines. The symbolic individual may be reverenced and placated like the Ainu bear, or he may be sacrificed. Frequently these developments occur together, for the human mind finds no difficulty in entertaining two or even more contradictory ideas. As a stage towards sacrifice we have, as in our childish games, many savage ceremonies in which men disguised as animals run around while the hunters pretend to kill them—a substitution of a living picture for a static representation. Then, though we frequently compare savages to children, we must remember that they have the passions and the physical capabilities of adult animals. Their pretence often passes into reality, and in times of stress the animalized man may be killed and eaten or distributed in lucky fragments, just as the original animal was in olden days. And this, in turn, may become a habit, and, when it becomes infected with a definite idea of appeasing hostile influences and powers, lead on to those periodic sacrifices of a human being endowed with divine or semi-divine attributes, which are so cheerfully described in Frazer's *Golden Bough*. We have no evidence of such sacrifices at present, but there is an allied belief that by eating parts of a man or by washing in his blood strength may be gained. " A Pondo chief in very olden days, on accession to the throne, would kill one of his brothers and wash in his blood to strengthen himself, and then would keep his medicines in the skull of the dead brother—a practice which raised the powers of the medicines to the nth as mathematicians would say " (Kidd). A set of drinking cups carved out of human skulls and ranged by some careful Magdalenian along the side of the cave of Le Placard may have been used for such a purpose. A Magdalenian youth had been buried in the Grotte des Hôteaux, near Roussillon, under suspicious circumstances, for, since his vertebræ and leg bones had been misplaced and transposed, it is clear that his flesh had been removed before burial. I mention such facts, though we cannot yet convict these tribes of human sacrifice. The flesh, for some obscure reason, *may* have been allowed to

D

rot from the bones; the skulls *may* have been taken from enemies slain in battle. But, though this animal cult is primarily concerned with man's universal prayer for his daily bread or flesh, there are two other cults that may already have mingled with this central stream of thought.

There is the reverence for the dead and the possibility of some rudimentary form of ancestor-worship. As far as I am aware, the most secret caves were not used as burial places, but we have some twenty Aurignacian burials in caves, and the three interments that can be assigned to the Magdalenian period show that the Aurignacian burial rites still continued. Of these, the remains of a man and parts of a woman found at Laugerie Basse had been protected with large stones and buried with cowries from the Mediterranean; a man and a woman at Obercassel had both been raddled and covered with great slabs of basalt; the Roussillon youth lay in a bed of red ochre, together with flints, pins and needles, a bâton with the carving of a stag upon it, and a girdle of three lion and forty-seven bear teeth, all of which were canines and some of which were engraved with seals and fishes. There is then a likelihood that even in the Old Stone Age some association might have arisen between the cave rites of the animal cult and any other rites which might cluster around cave burials. If this occurred the magician would, as the spiritual leader, hold burial and memorial services as well as rogation days and harvest festivals. But for lack of evidence I cannot press this point.

Again, I have so far dealt with the nutritive origins of

magic and interwoven with these, now in synthesis and now in antithesis, throughout all life and throughout all belief, we have the reproductive aspect of existence. In a hunting community it is vital that the herds of game should keep up to strength. Judging, however, by the illustrations of massed herds and by the abundant animal remains around the hearths, the danger that the food supply would decrease was less serious than a possibility that the tribe might run short of hunters. Rites that will increase the fertility of plants and animals hardly become important until hunters are driven into scarcity areas, become regrettably attached to some particular beast (like the well-known Witchetty Grub of Australia and other totems), or have begun to depend upon domestic plants and animals. At present the land was thickly stocked with game, but thinly peopled with men, and, moreover, the adult males would be constantly exposed to the dangers of the field. To make good the casualties, each hunter would have to keep his 'quiver' full, and any means, psychical as well as physical, would be used to attain this end. This old desire indeed still rules the stagnant minds of those who oppose birth-control and thereby look to the continuance of war and slum conditions. But in Aurignacian days the survival rate was probably a low one. Their statuettes may be interpreted as necessary symbols or goddesses of fertility, for in all of them, even though the extremities may taper off till the image looks like a spindle, the essentials remain, and in most of them great stress is laid upon maternity or an advanced stage of pregnancy. The female in the bas-relief at Laussel is one of the less marked examples, but she holds in her hand a bison's horn, notched like a hunter's tally—the Aurignacian cornucopia (Plate III.).

Among the definitely sexual representations there is at David in France a wall painting (described as Aurignacian) in which a number of ithyphallic men are followed by women. Amongst the portable objects found in the Aurignacian deposits we have a vulva from Montespan; another vulva carved on stone, together with a phallus of bison horn from Les Roches; a phallus engraved on reindeer horn, and a curious double specimen from Teyjat. These may be taken as precursors of the artificial phallus or *fascinum* that had, at times, a considerable vogue in Greece and Rome, and also appears in the witch cult of the West. Cowries, likewise, crop up both in Aurignacian and Magdalenian times, and since some have been brought from a considerable distance and others are carved in ivory, we can assume that they had even then their obvious significance as symbols of fertility. Even to-day in Southwark some considerate mothers still present their daughters at marriage with a cowry to avert 'ill luck,' and our sailors love to bring home large, pink-lipped shells.

In the Capsian art of Spain there is one interesting picture of nine women—the number is a familiar one—in skirts and conical head-dresses, grouped round a naked male figure, which is drawn on a slightly smaller scale and may have been an idol (Plate IV.). Taking palæolithic art as a whole, however, and having regard to the rarity of

PLATE III

THE MOST ANCIENT GODDESS KNOWN.

A bas-relief on a stone at the rock shelter of Laussel,
Dordogne, France. This figure and several statuettes represent
maternity; and the bison horn, which it holds, probably
stands for a 'horn of plenty.' Aurignacian Culture c. 14,000
—11,000 B.C. (Reduced from a photograph by Lalanne.
From Sollas, *Ancient Hunters*. Macmillan & Co.)

such objects and their occurrence in the most holy places, we can find little, if any, evidence of that pornography which is so marked a feature of our industrial civilizations. The older symbolism may, in fact, be interpreted on an economic rather than a Freudian basis.

In fertility cults, therefore, we have the second great stream which motivates early magical practices and religious beliefs, and which derives its power from the reproductive impulses of life. In it the women, as befits the fruitful half of the community, play a prominent part. Our other cult depends upon the nutritive and self-protective impulses of life, and is largely dominated by the adult males, especially in a hunting community. These two streams may run side by side, or their rites (especially those which concern fertilization rather than birth) will overlap, and a hint of this can be seen in the wounded animal below the Cogul women and in the masked but ithyphallic figure on Plate II. A single magician in a small community may have to play many parts. In later times the streams may separate widely, or they may fuse, or the fertility rites when they are applied to domestic plants and animals swell to such dimensions that those of the chase become vestigial and their trappings can then be seen as archaic wreckage that floats on a wider tide of custom. Unless, indeed, they assume new functions, like so many vestigial organs, and survive in the killing of men and in the magic of war.

Now, though we can, from our modern standpoint, analyze out and abstract the various ingredients in a savage belief, it by no means follows that these exist as separate entities in the mind of the savage himself. He feels and lives rather than thinks, and will not readily distinguish between the natural and the mystical aspects of some strange phenomenon. Both aspects, indeed, will leap into his brain at once, even as we do not pause to distinguish between the sound of the words which we hear and the meaning which they convey. Our scientific modes of thought render it difficult for us to recapture this frame of mind, since we have gradually come to lay more emphasis upon our secondary or natural laws of immediate cause and effect than upon the primary or supernatural causes which simpler minds will constantly apprehend. Thus science quarrels with magic and religion.

But though the mind of a savage is apt to appear confused and contradictory concerning the wider issues of his faith, here and there sharp details of individual practice and social ritual will emerge, the exact wording of a spell or of oral tradition, the correct cut or colour of some vestment, the things that must or must on no account be done. Such details will often fill the mental foreground of layman and priest alike to the exclusion of any general principles or wider aims. The main currents of a savage's belief flow strongly, but the tributaries that feed these streams lie in the distant hills and hidden springs that are beyond his ken. He rarely speculates upon them. Like Topsy, he is content that his belief and ritual 'just growed.' Later, when he begins to speculate, he seeks not to explain but, in tales and myths and legends, to explain

38

away customs whose origin has been forgotten, and at the same time to reinforce his magic by giving it some supernatural and unquestionable warranty. In this sense, therefore, myth, when it arises, "fulfils in primitive culture an indispensable function: it expresses, enhances, and codifies belief; it safeguards and enforces morality; it vouches for the efficiency of ritual and contains practical rules for the guidance of man" (Malinowski). Also, for lengthy periods myth will save men the trouble of thinking for themselves.

Perhaps these hunters had their myths, but what these were we cannot say. We can merely note this masked magician with his horns and tail, his primary control over food magic, and perhaps secondary functions connected with the disposal of the dead and the perpetuation of the living.

CHAPTER III

MAGICIANS AND PRIESTS

An age of transition—Why art declines—Conventional forms and
signs—The horned magician continues—The bull and the bee—
Wildigs and androgynes—The essential priest—The rôle of the
virile woman.

IT was formerly believed that there was a great break
between the cultures of the Old Stone Age and those of
the Neolithic or New Stone Age which are distinguished
by the presence of domestic food animals and plants. In
Europe, however, instead of a break we must recognize
the Middle Stone Age or Mesolithic period—'Epipalæo-
lithic' is a cumbrous term preferred by some writers
—with two outstanding cultures known as the Azilian
and the Tardenoisian, both of which were derived from
the Final Capsian cultures of Spain, though the earlier
Azilian deposits also show traces of Magdalenian influence.
This mesolithic period, which, according to the time-table
that I am using, lasted from about 7000 B.C. to 4000 B.C.,
is essentially one of transition. No hard and fast lines can
be drawn between the successive cultures; man still depends upon the wild products of nature; material progress
is only shown by the domestication of the dog and, at the
close of the period, by the pottery and partly polished tools
of the Shellheap peoples of the Baltic. The whole aspect
of the period is in fact one of continuity rather than change,

and while man's physical and psychological demands remain the same, in some areas, at least, I cannot doubt that the animal cult continued, although our evidence is of a fragmentary nature.

This is mainly because the pictorial art which enshrined the palæolithic beliefs degenerated rapidly, and this in turn is probably due to two causes, a climatic change and a change in the habits and the mental outlook of the more dominant races. In the first place, after a cold phase around 7000 B.C., the climate became progressively warmer and wetter, the reindeer moved northwards, and it is probable that the Magdalenians had, like the Eskimo, become so closely adapted to sub-arctic conditions that they moved with them, leaving only a few laggards or half-breeds to mingle with the eastward expansion of the Capsians from Spain. This would explain the complete disappearance of the Magdalenian art. Also a heavier rainfall rendered some of the caves, which are our museums, undesirable and even inaccessible. The Upper Magdalenian remains in the Mas d'Azil are, for example, separated from those of the Azilian culture by great flood deposits laid down by the subterranean stream. Some of the older artists were washed out of or cut off from their galleries, while at the same time the Capsians, an active folk, took increasingly to a more open life, which finally led to the encampments of the Tardenoisians, who, like the Solutreans, have left little behind them except their weapons. An early desertion of the wetter caves, therefore, and a more nomadic life in flimsy huts did not favour the production or the preservation

41

of enduring objects which would reveal the presence of the magician. None the less, the rites may have continued just as they do amongst the forest Indians of North America or the negroes of the veld, though, if these had lived in mesolithic times, nothing would remain of their animal paintings on skins, their vestments, instruments, or medicines. This applies equally to the longshore and rather poverty-stricken settlements on the Baltic. Bones also rot more easily in the open, and throughout the whole period only two skeletons belonging to the cultures which I have named have been found in the West. These lay in the Azilian layers at the Mas d'Azil cave, and both were rouged—lone witnesses to the palæolithic practice.

Under these adverse conditions I must first turn to the paintings of the Final Capsian culture in Spain, some of which, as Obermaier has shown, degenerate into purely conventional figures, and finally into crosses, pierced circles, and zigzags like those on the painted pebbles which mark the Azilian culture in France, Scotland, and Switzerland. Others in the Spanish caves, though they become stylistic and also conventional, remain recognizably human for a longer period. In Burkitt's opinion, many of these later figures were drawn in late neolithic and even eneolithic times, when metal tools were first finding their way into the South. If this opinion is accepted—and I see no reason why it should not be—a debased form of art, with representations of horned men and women, was carried over from the close of the palæolithic period to the Bronze Age in the wilder and drier caves of the sierras.

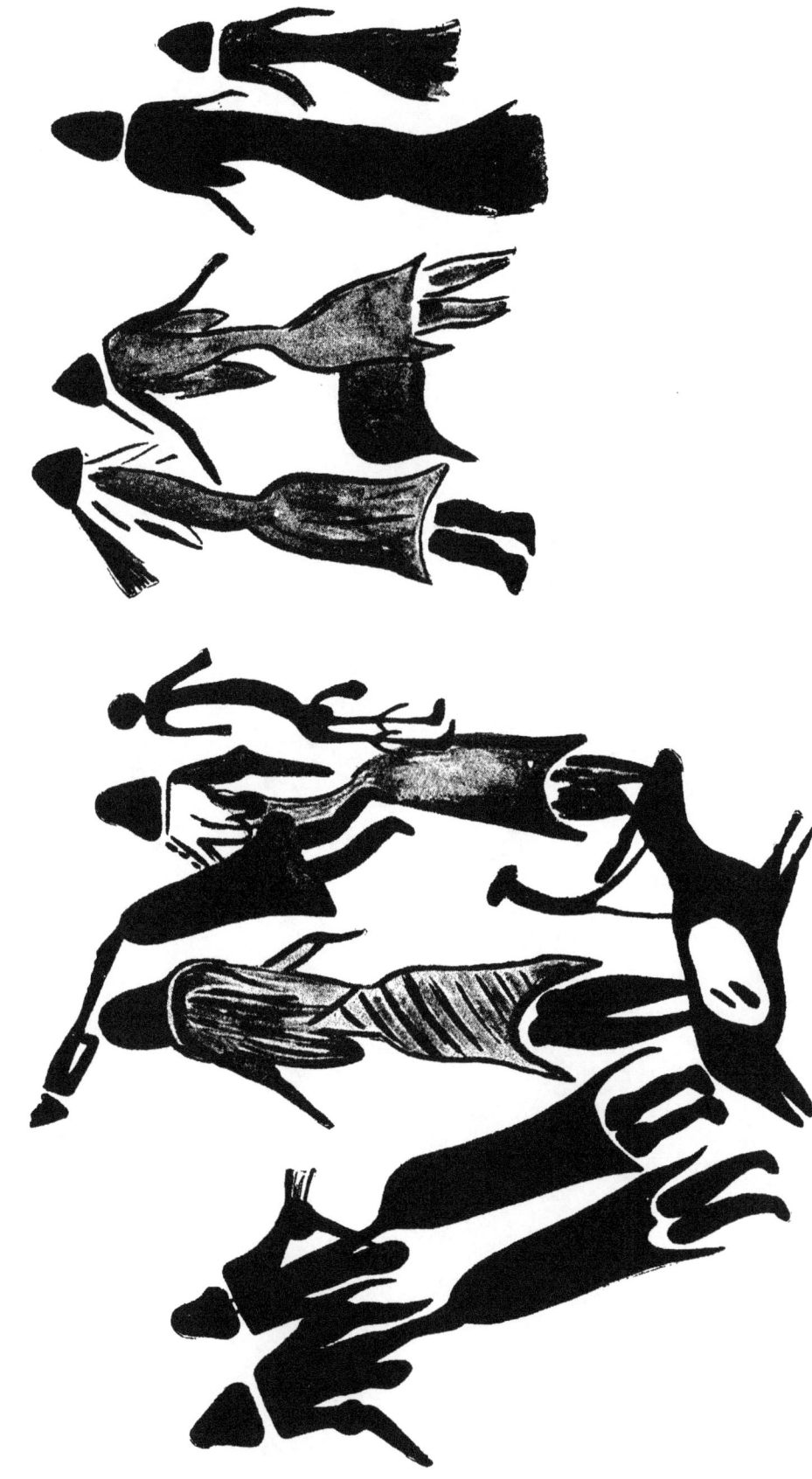

ANCIENT RITES IN SPAIN.

A painting made at Cogul, Lerida, Spain, about 9,000 years ago. Nine women with pendent breasts, clad in skirts and hats (the ordinary dress of the period), are posturing round a male figure. Late Capsian Culture, c. 8,000—7,000 B.C. (After Breuil and Cabre. Scale about ¼ actual size. A wounded deer is also shown. From MacCurdy, *Human Origins*. Appleton & Co.)

[*facing p.* 42

MAGICIANS AND PRIESTS

Of the Capsian paintings, I have already mentioned the Cogul dance (Plate IV.). There is also a wonderful frieze at Alpera, where we find hunting scenes, numerous small men with the bows and arrows (which the Capsians first introduced into Europe), and two figures which stand out by reason of their size, since one is about three times and the other about one and a half times larger than the ordinary mortals. The giant has a Wellingtonian nose and a Red Indian head-dress of many tall feathers, and is striding along in a most determined manner with his weapons; the other, who was drawn by the same hand between the giant's legs, is stampeding along in the same direction. Here we have obviously a chief, and on a smaller but none the less reputable scale his faithful magician; for the latter has a tufted tail, possibly that of a wild bull, an elongated head like that of a cat, which strongly suggests an animal visor, and is crowned with two tufts of straight lines, which may or may not be feathers. A few of the smaller hunters have horn-like appendages of a doubtful nature, but none have tails or transverse heads. This witch doctor is unmistakable, but now the art declines. I suggest a further cause. The more naturalistic Capsian paintings show us men collecting honey and being pestered by wild bees (that look like four-winged doves or top-heavy cherubs); men following a spoor; striding like the chief; tearing after wounded stags or—and this is significant—after wounded warriors. A premium is set upon swiftness; men are drawn with wisp-like bodies and enormous legs; hunting and battle scenes are frequent, and, apart from

43

magic, may have been drawn from commemorative rather than magical motives. Then such figures become still more debased; limbs and bodies being represented by mere lines, heads by dots or 'toasting-forks' (Fig. 2). A man's legs

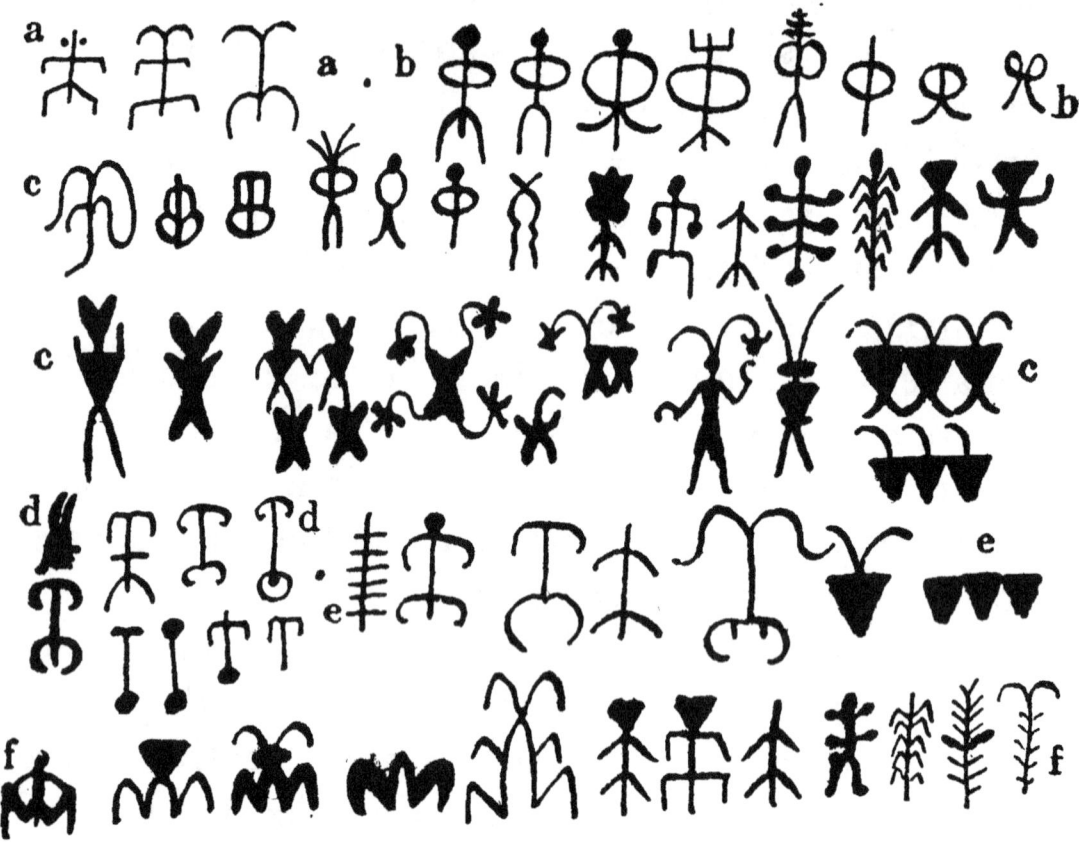

FIG. 2.—GENERALIZED HUMAN FIGURES FROM SOUTH SPAIN.

a, Figures that become 'cross-men' when they have lost their legs; *b,* a 'loop-man,' a 'loop-woman,' another 'loop-man,' a man and a woman with head-dresses, further degenerations. Figures that were probably masked are shown at *d* and near the middle of the second row from the top. The middle row contains figures with 'ears,' 'antennæ,' and the 'blobs,' that perhaps represent rattles; *f* shows a degeneration of squatting figures. These small rock paintings from various localities in South Spain range from the mesolithic and neolithic cultures to the dawn of the Bronze Age— *i.e.,* from *c.* 7000-2000 B.C. (After Breuil. From Sollas' *Ancient Hunters.* Macmillan and Co.)

may be drawn as a single line, so that, if his arms are outstretched, he becomes a cross; or, if they are akimbo, they become loops on either side of a straight line (Fig. 2, *b*). On a boundary stone at Clonfinlough, Ireland, a number of 'loop men' oppose a number of 'cross men,' an evident representation of a battle scene. Again, limbs may be omitted, so that a man is represented by a triangular body with or without a knob for a head; and women, who wore skirts, became sacks with vestigial limbs and heads, like the rag dolls of our nurseries. Obermaier has also traced a curious devolution from figures of men squatting in the attitude of a Cossack dance or a corroboree, to figures in which the body gradually disappears and the legs alone remain as a splayed-out M (Fig. 2, *f*). Several of these M's or crosses or triangles may be linked together to stand for some social or religious gathering. I cannot help associating this decline in Capsian and Azilian art with the adoption of a more active and warlike life, in which fertility rites would become more important than the simpler hunting rites. This is quite likely, because the tribal warfare, that is vividly illustrated in several paintings, would take a heavier toll of the male population, as the Capsians invaded the open lands. Lions and wolves were also numerous. Indeed, the life of an active hunter and warrior rarely favours art, and, at the same time, may beget a callousness which leads to a neglect of the dead, unless the victors turn themselves into sarcophagi. These points are illustrated in the advance of the Zulus against the more primitive negroes and the bushmen of South Africa, where we can see the same absence of pictorial art, a casual treatment of the dead, and magic concentrated upon the killing of enemies and rites which secure the fertility of the tribe and divest the women of any hankering after chastity, rather than upon hunting and the fertility of wild herds.

But, apart from this, we must recognize the general continuity of the mesolithic period, which, in turn, passes without any sudden changes through the 'Campignian' and other nebulous cultures into the neolithic civilizations, when a knowledge of agriculture and stock raising had filtered through from the dwellers on the Danube and the Swiss Lakes to the more favoured areas of the West. We can say quite vaguely that this neolithic phase lasts in Western Europe from about 4000 B.C. to 2500 B.C., when the first metal implements had begun to appear in Spain and France. The attention of archæologists has naturally turned to the richest neolithic settlements, and in these we find no trace of the magician, and must again explain his apparent absence. This is now due to the marked changes that follow when communities, using the best land, have found an assured food supply in the plants and animals which they have domesticated, and which, in turn, domesticate them. An animal can, for the first time (I except the mesolithic dogs), be controlled effectively, and thus much of the old respect for food animals may depart; or familiarity, if it does not breed contempt, begets a new outlook and raises the barrier that man begins to place between himself and the brute creation. When animal worship continues, it is now bent on preservation rather than destruction, and takes the form of rites to secure an increase. Or, again, the old animal cult, with its attendant practices, changes, so that the beast appears more and more in a symbolical aspect, as a totem or as a vehicle of some higher power. With the cultivation of grain man also acquires a staple and nutritious form of food that can be preserved, and this opens the avenues to the highest forms of social evolution. Still more attention is paid to fertility rites at seed-time and harvest, to exorcisms against crop pests, to rain-making and prayers for fine weather (though hunters and fishing folk indulge in these also when conditions are favourable, much as one of our bishops is said to have postponed all prayers for rain since the barometer was too high). But such crises at which magic must be employed are less frequent than the perpetual calamities which may befall the hunter. Magic becomes more intermittent, like a religion kept for Sundays. Also, though wealth and leisure quickly increase and more creative energy is set free, this energy is at first apt to be directed into material rather than religious channels. The early neolithic peoples had an enormous amount to learn and to invent. They had to face new and pressing problems at every turn; many of which—like a reluctant motor-car— would best be solved by intellectual and scientific thought rather than by emotional desire and cajolery. Man must learn to cultivate, to pasture, and protect his beasts. He invents new tools, receptacles, and storehouses; he builds better dwellings, polishes his tools, learns to weave and to embroider. We get the very practical outlook that is shown by the cultures of the Swiss lake-dwellers (though there I suspect that we are also dealing with a different racial mentality), in which no burials or grave goods have been found and the only objects which may have had a magical significance are a few clay models of ox horns. The same 'worldly' preoccupation occurs again in the early history of our colonies and America, where men for a while may be too busily engaged in utilizing new lands to produce any great works of art or large religious monuments, though they may come to excel in the advancement of applied science. But, though fertility rites would in time dominate the more progressive agricultural and pastoral communities, one must realize that over large areas the people still lived by hunting, especially in wild, hilly regions, which even to-day remain as game preserves and as the home of primitive and backward peoples. In these the older cults would thrive, and we have also our evidence from the dry caves of Spain (Fig. 2).

I will not produce the simple 'cross men' or the 'loop men,' for though some have heads like forks, the prongs most probably stand for ordinary plumes. Similarly, other bodies are reduced to thick vertical lines, sometimes prolonged between the legs, which, like the arms, are drawn as thick curved lines. Such figures, two horseshoes linked at their centres by a bar, also occur on pebbles belonging to the Azilian culture, where they may be still further reduced by the loss of the arms to a mere two-pronged fork. But in the more complete cave painting (Fig. 2, *d*), which may, therefore, possibly belong to an earlier or, at

48

least, wilder, mesolithic phase, we see, above this body, and separated from it by a narrow neck, the head of some large animal with two distinct horns. Another 'panto-mime' mask, with three blunter protuberances instead of the horns, surmounts a similar body in the second row of Fig. 2, just below the largest loop man. The age of most of these degenerate figures is uncertain; some may be mesolithic, others are assigned to neolithic and eneo-lithic times, when metals began to be used. Amongst them one can also see well-drawn figures of men with two long, thin antennæ rising from their heads, and then more de-based figures, sometimes mere triangles and M's with similar antennæ, which irresistibly recall the conventional-ized horns of Mephistopheles and the appendages given to gnomes, brownies, and elves by the illustrators of our fairy-tales. These antennæ often end in curious blobs, for which I can offer no explanation unless they represent rattles containing pebbles, like those which Bushmen still wear to accentuate the rhythm of their dances, and which survive in the jester's bladder of peas and the bells attached to his person, and to Morris dancers.

Some of these blobs have two stumpy 'wings,' or four wings, which fan out like a child's drawing of a moth. If I may be allowed to digress for a moment, they remind me of the Capsian rendering of bees, the heraldic *fleur-de-lys* (which almost certainly originated as a bee, and was not derived from an iris, a spear-head, or a palm-tree), and the fact that in early days bees were the source of sweetness, wax, and mead. I can hardly suggest that such vague, isolated blobs stood for *Apis mellifica;* but if they ever did so, it is interesting to recall the ancient association of the bee with the Apis bull in Egypt; with various Greek and Roman deities, such as Apollo and Mellona; with the Delphic oracle; with Mithras worship; and with Childeric I., whose tomb contained the golden head of a bull and about three hundred golden bees. The bee then appears on the arms of the Popes and on the robes of Charlemagne and Napoleon, as it had once done on the crown of the Pharaohs of Lower Egypt. More curious was the widespread and persistent belief that bees could be engendered in the bodies of dead oxen, which we find, for example, in Vergil's recipe and reflected in Samson's experience with the lion. Also in Christian myth this small *ancilla domini*, or handmaid of the lord, apart from her appearance in the respectable company of St. Ambrose, has for her patron an obscure bishop with the suspicious name of Saturninus, who was appropriately martyred by means of a maddened bull in the heresy-haunted, or rather the pagan, city of Toulouse. But to return to the caves.

Amongst the late figures we find some with triangular bodies and triangular heads, the corners of which are prolonged into a pair of ears (or horns) like those of an ass or a jester (Fig 2, *c*). Though we cannot be certain—and we can be still less certain when these forms, and the antennæ types, dwindle into shapes like a double cusp or a dice-box—a comparison with some Bushman drawings of 'antelope men' leaves the impression that the magician is still with us. Some of these also, instead of having bare legs, are sack-like in form and may well be witches, since we have other sack-like, but hornless, figures in the caves which have been called female idols, and the neolithic or eneolithic 'statue menhirs' in France, which are definitely female, and are clad in long robes and fringed bands that give them a strangely ecclesiastical appearance.

Since I intend to follow the more primitive cult, I can only refer briefly to the more advanced civilizations of the Neolithic and the Bronze Ages. In these the old magician, as such, seems to have been overlaid or ousted by beliefs that are now enregistered in dolmens, passage-graves, vast tumuli, and megalithic monuments, and by a host of gods and goddesses derived in part, at least, from the ancient civilizations of the East. His influence can, no doubt, be traced in all these cults and creeds, but I do not propose to depart from the Western area; and so, leaving all the fauns and satyrs from their simplest forms to their apotheosis in the great god Pan, I must wait till the Iron Age cultures for further evidence.

But before I proceed to historic times, and while, in fact, we can still see the wood for the trees, I will venture upon some remarks about the nature of the magician himself, or, if you like, the 'inner voice' which led him to serve the tribe in his peculiar capacity.

If we take an infant tadpole we find that its sex seems to remain indeterminate for a fairly long period, which we may speak of as a hermaphrodite stage; after which one set of sex organs matures, while the other set remains rudimentary, so that the adult frogs are either predominantly male or predominantly female. In the lowly frog, however, and rather frequently in certain toads, the bisexuality of youth sometimes lingers on into the adult stages, and we find casual but true hermaphrodites. In higher animals, such as human beings, matters may not go to these lengths, and yet in some individuals, though one sex is predominant, we have more or less emphatic hints that the other sex has not been as fully suppressed as it might be. Actually it has been shown that in mammals, and in some insects, the factors which determine sex are present in the fertilized egg; but it would seem that they may vary in potency, that during development one factor may not succeed in duly controlling the other. This is beautifully illustrated by some abnormal specimens of moths and butterflies, in which the wings on one side show the coloration of the male, while those on the other side show the contrasting colours of the female; and by some scarab beetles, when one can easily collect a series in which the enormous horns that decorate the head and thorax of a normal male show a gradual diminution until some, though true males, can barely be distinguished by these secondary sexual characters from an unusually knobby or masculine type of female. Incidentally, some scarabs stand on the lowest rung of the social ladder in that, unlike most insects, the males help the females to provide for the family, and the long-lived females protect their young until they have reached maturity. In such insects secondary sex characters are possibly affected by differences in nutrition; and in truly social insects we have the regular occurrence of the sterile (or normally sterile) female workers amongst ants and bees and the approximate male and female castes of workers and soldiers amongst the termites, wherein we can see a physical response, enforced by nurture, to the demands of a complex civilization.

The vertebrates have not yet reached this stage, or, in the case of man, with his unspecialized body but highly evolved brain, respond on the mental rather than the physical plane to similar demands; and yet we can often note both physical and mental approximations between the sexes in the higher social animals and in those whose natural equilibrium has been upset by the more severe forms of domestication. The farmer is well acquainted with that portent of ill-luck, an elderly crowing hen; with the 'free martin,' an ungainly and barren cow, that always occurs as a twin to a bull calf; while 'wildig' is an old term for an abnormality in which, though the young beast looks exactly like a female, maturity reveals the presence of male impulses, and, in addition to the female organs, an incomplete and hidden set of male organs. Crew states that the wildig is by far the commonest form of an approximation between the sexes in goats and pigs. The causes of such abnormalities are obscure. Some are doubtless present in the egg, and, like other innate weaknesses that lead to freaks, their occurrence may be rendered more common by the unnatural conditions that attend domestication; and man is the most domesticated of all animals. In birds and mammals also the full realization or dominance of one sex factor over the other depends

53

upon the quantity and, according to Steinach, the quality of definite secretions from the ductless glands. In a young male these secretions, on the one hand, stimulate the development of his sex organs, and, on the other hand, check the development of female organs. In a female, of course, it is the other way round. Thus, the free martin is believed to have been adversely influenced in the womb by secretions that she has absorbed from her bull twin; and in man it is a common belief that a girl twin to a boy will never have children. Other abnormalities may also be assigned to natural variations in the size and activity of the glands concerned and to unnatural variations caused by injury or disease. Next, at puberty, secretions from the sex organs (probably interacting with further streams from the ductless glands) control the development of the secondary characters proper to each sex, and, until their activities cease, check the latent characters of the opposite sex. This is amply illustrated by the capon, the squeaky, beardless eunuch, or the more resourceful spider crabs and campion plants that, after castration by parasites, may develop productive ovaries. I have been unable to verify the account of a duck who was run over by a motor and thereafter functioned as a drake; but there is in the British Museum a Tiresian hen who, when she could no longer perform her wifely duties, took upon herself those of a cock and became the father of several broods of healthy chicks.

These, of course, are extreme examples, but they serve to emphasize the fact that either a man or a woman may have an undue proportion of the opposite sex in his or her mentality. This may be due to nature, to nurture, to injury, or to age. In the latter event, it is the women, with their earlier climacteric, who so often assume secondary male characters and that increased desire for domination which is a source of so much discomfort and the subject of infinite jest. The latent female in a normal man is less in evidence because his reproductive period is longer; his secondary male characters, like those of a salmon or a stag, become intensified with age; and any characters such as gentleness, guile, religiosity, or an unusual fondness for children, which might in his old age reveal the female element, are apt to be masked by symptoms of senility or some last erotic flicker which has to be hushed up by his relatives. This time factor, then, partly explains why witches are usually represented as hags and why the masculine type of woman is more common than the feminine type of man, who, in his essential form, would seem to be the result of some innate weakness, however much he may also owe to early environmental influences, such as the tyranny of a doting mother, and in our complex societies to physical or mental castration and specialized forms of suggestion and miseducation.

It is this feminine type of male that I would identify in primitive societies with the true magician. But not all feminine males. Extreme cases, like the human wildigs that one sometimes meets, would probably have been drowned by any self-respecting tribe while they were still girls, so to say; and pusillanimous, weak-kneed examples are usually reduced to the status of slaves or barren squaws.

But less marked examples occur, and these, though they may have a poor physique, a less stable mentality, and no great love for manly sports or warlike exercises, often have, by reason of their bisexual outlook, a stereoscopic view of life, a quick intelligence, cunning, tenacity, patience, and a power of opportune adaptation, together with a strong desire for self-expression. In fact, they often have an unusually large amount of ambition and emotional energy, which cannot, of course, be expressed in motherhood and may not find an adequate outlet in paternity, since their proper sexual impulses are apt to be weak or confused or restrained by various conventions. They are, indeed, lustful rather than lusty fellows, and somewhat disconsolate. Like the eunuchs of the East, they may foment rebellions against the chief, but there is in a primitive community one legitimate channel for their activity—the need for organized magic and the need for professed magicians. This is the niche of opportunity for the feminine male, who, in addition to brains, also possesses an impressive personality. We have, as in all evolution, the impulse towards, or the desire for, self-expression and self-realization on the one hand, and an unoccupied gap in the environment or elbow room in the social system on the other. The *vis a tergo* and the *vis a fronte*. Amongst a number of 'square' hunters the rounded magician slips into a round hole.

As a comment upon this view I may take the statement that the magician amongst the aborigines of Australia has no powers other than those which he can gain by the

exercise of his own personality; and the neurotic performances of the Red Indian medicine-men and the shamans
of the North. Kidd's note on the Zulus puts the matter
plainly, for, as he says, "the ranks of the diviners or
doctors are recruited mainly from the more intelligent and
clever members of the tribe. To be a successful doctor a
man must have keen powers of observation, a good supply
of mother-wit, and an endless stock of barefacedness. As
a rule, he has a neurotic tendency and is predisposed to see
visions and dream vivid dreams. In a word, he must be
susceptible to psychic influences." It is this predisposition
that will first bring the child to the notice of the magicians,
whereupon, should he be regarded as a likely candidate,
he is subjected to a severe training, which will strengthen
his original bias. Then, if he survives, he is initiated into
the various rites and ceremonies.

Frequently, of course, a chief may also act as a magician
and officiate at the greater ceremonies, or, like Chaka and
Henry VIII., claim a nominal supremacy for political or
economic reasons; but I would maintain that the essential
magician, from an inspired leader to an everyday practi-
tioner, is an exceptional person whose vocation has been
determined by his mixed mentality. Even when such a
man arises in a ruling family, his neurotic tendencies will
in the long run be a hindrance to his success as a warlord.
In a savage society he cannot be a chieftain; he is unwilling
to be an ordinary subject; magic remains the only field in
which he can employ his talents.

Under the same conditions the position of a woman with

a masculine nature, a strong personality, and a good brain
is even more invidious. She will not be satisfied with the
ordinary pursuits of the tribal women or the petty malice
of the village gossip. She may, for physical and mental
reasons, be unable to employ the usual devices by which
ambitious women gain control over the leading men. Her
way to open political or religious domination is barred by
the male chiefs and magicians, especially in active and
warlike tribes, who are apt to enforce some kind of Salic
law. Her position is unfortunate; but, since this type occurs
rather frequently, some individuals emerge from time to
time, such as the female witch doctors of the negroes
or those warrior-queens—Mæve, Brunhild, Boadicea,
" tall and forbidding, keen of eye and harsh of voice "—
who ride through the early history of the Nords. A curious
parallel was observed in the troop of baboons that I mentioned before, which, instead of having a single 'king,'
" was dominated by a council of old males and one barren
homosexual female (with secondary male characteristics)."
Where masculinity is the result of age we have also the
dominance that is often gained by an old hen, a bellwether,
the elder wapiti and antelope cows, who usually lead the
herd, or the procession of our own cows back from the
pasture, when the more experienced matrons often insist
in a most human and vicious manner upon their rights of
precedence. Warrior-queens are, however, rare in most
races in which the men and women lead very different
lives, and more usually such androgynes take to illicit
practices as witches. In higher or, at least, more compli-

cated civilizations I still believe that these remarks about the nature of magicians and witches—or, in allowed religions, priests and priestesses—hold good, though they must be qualified. Allowances must be made for the inclusion of less gifted individuals who act as subordinates or lay brethren. Again, in cults where the magician must run the risk of being sacrificed periodically to his own god and for his people, we find substitutes who are accorded divine honours for a certain period. In theocracies and state religions, or national creeds that are little more than codes, I need hardly say that numerous men and women of high and low degree will also assume a religious life from political, economic, or parasitic motives; and others are thrust into it, lest they become a nuisance to, or a burden upon, their relatives.

But under all the complexities of historic times we still find those 'inspired' visionaries who prefer the emotional path of the magician and priest to the more purely intellectual professions, even when these are open to the laity. And, more especially, I have to trace the Stone Age cults and the primitive beliefs of men amongst the witches and the superstitions of the ruder peasantry.

CHAPTER IV

THE HORNED GOD OF THE WEST

Racial ways of thought—The lord of the underworld—Cernunnos and his horns—A wife for a god—Diana and Hecate—Norse deities —Heimdal and Giant Grim—The strands of human belief— New gods for old—The truth in a fairy-tale.

WHEN we reach the Iron Age cultures some mention must be made of the three dominant races of Europe and their distinct types of mentality. For during this period we have the westward extension of the tall, fair, long-headed Nordic Race, which had left the Russian steppes and had already conquered the round-headed members of the Alpine Race in Central Europe, and then appeared in France, and also concentrated in the Baltic and Scandinavian lands. The aborigines of the West mainly belonged to the dark, long-headed Mediterranean Race, which still holds its own in our Celtic-speaking areas and in the Iberian Peninsula, together with remnants of the Old Stone Age races in poorer or more mountainous regions like the Dordogne, the Pyrenees, and parts of Wales. We are confronted, then, in the best lands by an amalgam of races. There are the Nordic conquerors, who as steppe-folk and warriors inclined to sun cults with their symbolic wheels, solstitial fires, sun chariots drawn by horses or swans, and to patriarchal warlike deities. There are the

60

Alpine and Nordic-Alpine crosses with a practical rather than an emotional outlook which, in the concrete, found its expression in the *lares* and *penates* of the homestead; and, in the abstract, led to the more intellectual and less ornate doctrines of the Reformation. Lastly, we have the emotional, less stable, but ingenious Mediterraneans, who gave great prominence to female deities; to cunning gods like Mercury and Bacchus, who outwitted the Nordic gods; to a host of lesser and local demi-gods; and, with that remarkable concentration upon a material existence after death which we see in ancient Egypt and in the Catholic Church, to a deity who presided over a most real world of ghosts and demons. Valerius Maximus even states that a Celt would lend money on a promissory note redeemable in the world to come. As, indeed, men do in a vaguer sense to-day.

In pre-Christian times, then, there were many creeds and cults, and classical writers refer to a number of Celtic and Gallic gods. The word 'Celtic,' however, is most confusing. A French anthropologist usually refers to the short, dark members of the Alpine Race in the West. An Englishman thinks of the dark, mercurial members of the Mediterranean Race in Wales and parts of Ireland and Scotland. While some of the *Celtæ* and *Galati*, described by Greeks and Romans as tall blondes, undoubtedly belonged to the Nordic Race. It seems to have been these Nords who, in their first conquests, imposed their Aryan Gaelic and Brythonic tongues upon the Alpines and Mediterraneans, whose own languages, with the possible exception of Basque, are no longer spoken in Europe. The 'Celtic' divinities, therefore, may include not only the Nordic but many Alpine, primitive Mediterranean, and even palæolithic deities, who often continued to live side by side, like the medley of gods upon Olympus, with a fair degree of intrigue and amiability. Tolerance for another man's belief had not yet been proscribed as a heinous sin.

In seeking the more primitive elements we may pass over the upper layer of beliefs which centred round the sun, the war gods, and similar deities akin to Apollo, Jupiter, and Mars. We may also leave the various 'Matres' of the Gauls, who probably absorbed the Aurignacian mother cult, but were now mainly concerned with the harvest rather than the fertility of man; though they sometimes dallied with a god of the underworld.

It is, indeed, in the underworld, in the lowest and oldest layer of belief that we must search; and here we find Dis, who was the Western equivalent of Pluto, god of the dead. Cæsar writes that the Gauls all claimed descent "*ab Dis patre*"—a claim which often shows us that we are dealing with a primeval god—but adds that they especially worshipped Mercury, being led, I believe, to this identification by the presence of some indigenous god who, like Mercury, led the souls of the dead to Hades. In the mixed mythologies of Greece and Rome we may note for future reference that Mercury was born in Arcadia; stole the oxen tended by Apollo; became the messenger of the gods; served Jove as a cup-bearer and also aided him in his surreptitious love affairs. All these traits recall the attitude of an aboriginal but intelligent race towards its conquerors; or that of a tout meeting an English tourist at some southern port. Mercury also possessed the hat of darkness, which could render him invisible, and was given the caduceus staff with the entwined serpents, which is more legitimately associated with Æsculapius and is now the badge of the Army Medical Corps. One of the epithets attached to him is Tricephalos, 'three-headed.'

I will now turn to some remains in France of the La Tène period, which lasted from about 500 B.C. and on into the time of the Roman occupation. The first of these is an altar stone that was dug up at Paris. In the centre we find a clothed and bearded figure with two stag's antlers growing from his head. From each of these hangs a torque, one of the twisted rings of gold which were used by the Celts as ornaments, as a form of currency, and as a symbol of wealth. The name Cernunnos is inscribed above the figure and can be derived from the Irish and Welsh *corn*, with the Latin *cornu*, in English, a *horn*. It obviously refers to this horned personage and also occurs on a tablet found at Pesth in the mention of a *funerary* college which held its meetings at the temple of Jupiter Cernenus. 'Jupiter' in this case would be merely a honorific applied to some underworld deity corresponding to the Jupiter Stygius of the Romans. The rest of the block is badly mutilated, but the head and shoulders of Cernunnos are on such a large scale compared to some smaller figures on either side that he obviously could not have been standing or even sitting, but was probably squatting with his legs crossed like a Buddha.

Thus a monument found at Rheims shows us the horned god squatting on a seat between Apollo and Mercury, who have to stand. From a bag held in the crook of his left arm he pours out a stream of acorns and beech-mast that falls between the attentive figures of an ox and a stag, which are carved beneath him. Another stone from Vendœuvres-en-Brenne represents the god with a sack in his lap and two diminutive figures on either side, who stand on the coils of a serpent and hold on to the horns of the god with one hand, while their free hands display a torque and a purse respectively.

One more of these monuments calls for comment. This was found at Saintes, and is unusual in that it presents two groups carved back to back on the opposite faces of the stone. On both faces a squatting god holds a torque and a purse or bag, which rests on his knee. The monument is imperfect and the god's horns are missing, but he may be identified with the figures that we have already seen. On the principal face, a female, with a cornucopia and a smaller female attendant, is sitting near the god. The other side of the block shows him squatting on a pedestal ornamented with two ox horns; to the left on a base with a single ox horn we have a naked god supporting himself on a club; to the right a goddess in a long robe stands on a plain base.

Sir John Rhys, who has reviewed these figures and a

statuette from Autun, identifies them with the Celtic Dis, the god of the underworld. Like Pluto, also, this Dis-Cernunnos, by his torque, was the god of wealth; and just as 'Pluto' is related to the Greek '*ploutos*,' meaning 'wealthy,' so Dis may be a contracted form of *Dives*. But though Cernunnos is the Western equivalent of the Greco-Roman Ades-Pluto, we cannot regard him as a late importation. For, as Rhys points out, he is antique both in his dress and in his attitude; and the " younger gods cluster round him like children by the side of their father." He adds : " All the facts at our disposal tend to show that the chthonian deity of the Celts and Teutons was held to have the form of a horned beast, such as a stag, bull, goat, or ram, and it is now needless to show why one cannot accept the conventional cornucopia as an adequate explanation of that idea. At the same time, it would be rash to say that they had no connection with one another, for the usual account of the *Cornu Copiæ*, or horn of plenty, traces it back to the Greek *keras Amaltheias*, or horn of the goat Amaltheia, from which Zeus was nourished, and in which also was to be found all that one could desire. Here we have also a horned beast older than Zeus, and the form of the myth does not compel us to assume that the goat was originally regarded as a she-goat; so it is possible that the Amalthæan goat and the horned deities are to be referred to a common origin." He says later, " that a divinity like Cernunnos should end his career by being absorbed into the incongruous character of the devil seems just what one might have expected."

THE HISTORY OF THE DEVIL

At this point I stop to see in Cernunnos the old palæolithic magician of the caves. In this cult he has been deified as a god of the dead, and, since the discovery of metals, probably by wild hunters in the old bare rocks of the hills, as a god of wealth. But he is still the progenitor of all men. He still encourages wild animals, the stag and the ox, or, rather, the auroch. Ancient of days, he stands aloof from the younger gods.

These points can again be illustrated by an octagonal silver caldron from Gundestrup in Jutland. The outside is decorated with the busts of four stern, bearded men and four forbidding females, war gods and their consorts, I presume. The inner plaques represent groups of cavalry and infantry, hunting scenes—the base is a bull hunt—but one is devoted to Cernunnos (Plate V.). Here inside the bowl he squats, like a good shikari, crowned with antlers and holding a torque, while his left hand grasps a serpent firmly by its neck. On his right a stag regards him, and on his left a wolf and a beast that may be a lion. The rest of the panel is filled in with a dubious goat, two ramping heraldic beasts, and a man riding a dolphin, which, like an elephant and three led unicorns on another plaque, may be due to foreign craftsmanship.

But what comes to the fore is the rôle of the magician as god of the dead. In some countries we may have the abode of the dead lodged in the sky; in the West we do have legends about the isles of the blest beyond the sunset's glow. But more often, and when men still believed that the earth was flat and extended to limitless depths

66

PLATE V

CERNUNNOS, THE GALLIC GOD.

Two plaques from a silver vase found at Gundestrup, Jutland, Denmark. The upper plaque shows Cernunnos holding a torque as a symbol of wealth and grasping the neck of a serpent. A stag and a wolf regard him. The lower plaque depicts cavalry and infantry and some myth or rite. Iron Age culture of La Tène, which lasted from about B C. 500 and on into Gallo-Roman times. (After Muller. From MacCurdy. *Human Origins*, Appleton & Co.)

beneath their feet, we have the idea that the dead descended into some underground world, where, with the possible exception of a few outrageous malefactors, they continued to live much as they had done on earth. This location of Hades would naturally follow upon the simple method of interment in the earth; would be strengthened by the old cave burials; and maintained by the later Western methods in which artificial sepulchres, dolmens, and passage-graves replaced the natural cave. The memories of cave rites still endure when heroes pass through caves to reach their dead, or pilgrims still visit famous holes like that of ‘ St. Patrick’s Purgatory ’ at Lough Dearg. And just as the palæolithic men supplied their dead with a lump of iron pyrites and some flints, so, I am informed, some Catholics in the Isle of Wight still place a candle and a box of matches in the coffin. In the Greek Hades ghosts flutter and squeak like bats; even the waters of Styx and Phlegethon may be the memory of subterranean streams barring an entrance or lit by the Magdalenian lamps and flaming torches when the old worshippers pushed on to the inmost sanctuary. Who, then, can be more appropriate as lord of this underworld than the old horned magician with his cult of the stag and the bull? And thus I believe Cernunnos came to be god of Hades, where the dead continued their lives as upon earth, until the post-Homeric distinction arose between Elysium and Tartarus; and the Christian, following Eastern creeds, set the infernal regions apart as the abode of the devils and the damned.

I will note one other peculiarity of underworld gods

that can be seen in a statuette from Autun. Here Cernunnos squats with one torque round his neck and another in his lap, while his hands hold apart two serpents, each of which has a ram's head. His horns have been lost, though the sockets for them remain. But in this figure, in addition to the one principal face, a spot above each of his ears is carved into a small face, so that he could look sideways as well as forwards. Other monuments give him three faces of equal size or three distinct heads; or, lastly, the triple head alone may suffice, and the lower part of the panel is used for his associates.

Of this development I will only say that the threefold way of looking at things is most marked amongst the Mediterraneans, who, rather than the uncultured and warring Nords, were mainly responsible for the art and magic of the West. A threefold motive continually occurs in the 'Celtic' art and ornament of the La Tène period, and in the old poems and spells of Wales and Ireland; it is sublimated in these three-headed gods of the underworld, and, lastly, in trinities of good and evil (Fig. 3).

Rhys here remarks that " this strange god reduced to a wonderful head, which identifies him with Janus, the Roman god of beginnings and endings, has his counterpart in Welsh tradition." He refers to the tale of Bran; but I must look to Janus or Dianus, another ancient and shadowed god who presided over generation, war, and the gates through which prayers found their way to the gods. He was two-faced. Sometimes he holds a bunch of keys, like Pluto, and according to one myth was the son of

Hecate. Amongst the Romans, the Kalends, or first day of each month, was sacred to Janus, and more particularly the kalends and the ninth day of January, a reckoning

FIG. 3.—THE TRINITY OF EVIL.

From a French manuscript of the fifteenth century in the Bibliothèque Royale, Paris. The artist has depicted a three-faced devil with antlers and a horned sceptre. He is chained to his throne in accordance with the desires of the period. (From Carus' *History of the Devil*. Open Court Publishing Co.)

based on the archaic nine-night week. There may also be some confusion between Janus, an Etruscan 'Diana,' or TH ANNA, and even an old Basque god called Jannicot.

With Rhys and other authorities, I must dismiss the old suggestion that in the three-headed gods of the West we merely find a late naturalization of the Roman Janus. They bear the native stamp of antiquity. We even have that palæolithic 'Cerberus.' There is, instead, the constant suggestion that the similarities which we find are due to a common origin. The more polished gods of the urban civilizations are meeting their country cousins. Rhys presumes that Mercury was associated with Cernunnos on the monuments because Mercury was the genius of commerce and money-making (but I would also see that Mercury who was death's messenger and had three heads), while the Gaulish Apollo was especially connected— English tourists are sometimes shocked when they encounter St. Apollinaris—with health-giving mineral springs, which rise from Cernunnos' realm.

Much might be written about the serpent: its wide acceptance in Africa and elsewhere as the messenger of death; its habit of emerging from the ground, sometimes near a burial-place, whereupon the Zulus will look upon it as the backbone or the entrails or in some way the spirit of the dead man; its habit of sloughing its skin, so that it seems reborn to health and strength; its emergence after hibernation, like its Gallic associate, the snail, with congruous ideas of resurrection; its tenacious hold on life; its rôle in the Garden of Eden; its power both to repel and to fascinate; its phallic significance . . . but I will spare the reader.

The problem of the female figures is more difficult. As

a god of the underworld, I can find no evidence that Cernunnos ever had a regular female consort; like Pluto, all the goddesses may have misliked his home. Perhaps I may divide the more primitive cults in which women are interested into three classes—those which concern birth; those of a virile goddess served by her Amazons; those which concern begetting. The first we have seen in the Old Stone Age, and Flinders Petrie has tried to show that the benignant goddess with the cornucopia at Saintes is derived from the Aurignacian female with her bison horn and is also " the predecessor of a deity found from Thrace to North Russia at the present day." An identification which would support that of Cernunnos with the magician. But, as any father knows, birth, with its strange and ancient rituals, is a business from which the male is excluded by the old midwives of the tribe. These, however, are sometimes dominant females, so that we may find a connection between the goddess of birth and a virile goddess, who, like an able old maid, may take an interest in infant welfare. We can see this in the mysteries of Diana Cybele, who, though she is generally represented as a robust and matronly female in an advanced stage of pregnancy, was suckled by wild beasts, and is at times confused with a celibate goddess.

Indeed, a fitting mate for Cernunnos would have been Diana, the Diana who was the savage goddess of hunting rather than the moon goddess, or Diana Cybele, or that 'animated pinecone' worshipped at Ephesus. The reason why she was not his constant spouse can best be shown by a pithy extract from Lemprière's *Classical Dictionary*, an excellent mine for the anthropologist, in that, like the legends of the saints, it contains much matter which is apocryphal, but none the less represents the thought of man : ". . . the pains, which she saw her mother suffer during her labour, gave her such an aversion to marriage, that she obtained from her father permission to live in perpetual celibacy, and preside over the travails of women; to shun the society of men, she devoted herself to hunting, and was always accompanied by a number of chosen virgins, who, like herself, abjured marriage; is represented with a quiver and dogs, sometimes in a chariot drawn by two white stags; sometimes appears with wings, holding a lion in one hand, a panther with the other, with a chariot drawn by 2 heifers, or 2 horses of different colours; represented taller by the head than her attendant nymphs; her face has something manly, her legs are bare, well-shaped and strong, and her feet covered with a buskin, worn by huntresses, among the ancients; received many surnames, particularly from places where her worship was established and from the functions over which she presided; called Ilythia, Lucina, or Juno Pronuba, invoked by women in child-bed, and Trivia, worshipped in cross-ways, where her statue was generally erected; was supposed to be the same as the Moon, and Proserpine or Hecate, and hence called Triformis; some of her statues represented her with 3 heads, that of a horse, dog, and boar . . . she is generally known in the figures which represent her, by the crescent on her head, the dogs which attend her, and her hunting habit." In this we can see the virile woman, but, none the less, "the favours, which she granted to Pan and Orion are well known." Her other names of Hecate and Proserpina—one may recall the myth of Pluto and Proserpina (Kore)—may lead us to infer that a Western Diana may have accorded like favours to Cernunnos. Strabo tells us that "in an island close to Britain, Demeter and Kore are venerated with rites similar to the orgies of Samothrace," an island in which we find the obscene mysteries of Cybele and her castrated Corybantes, those of the Cabiri and those of Hecate. Hecate herself was a repulsive female with the head of a dog, or the heads of a horse, a dog, and a boar, who presided over magic and enchantments. She appears as a stranger in Greek mythology, and may well have been a female derivative from the magician and the older prototype of Diana in her less endearing moods.

The last cult, which we saw in the Cogul dance, is one in which female adepts and initiates would play an important, but subordinate, rôle, as mistresses rather than matrons, and one which would not be depicted in these more civilized days. Dionysius of Halicarnassus does say that rites were performed by women on islands near to Guernsey and Jersey in honour of 'Bacchus,' whatever that may mean. Or we may see an echo of such rites, despite the mention of virginity, in an account by Pomponius Mela of the Breton isle of Sein: "Sena, in the Britannic Sea and opposite the coasts of the Osismi, is famous for its oracle of a Gaulish god, whose priestesses, living in the holiness of perpetual virginity, are said to be nine in number. They call them Gallizenæ, and they believe them to be endowed with extraordinary gifts, to rouse the sea and the wind by their incantations, to turn themselves into whatsoever animal form they may choose, to cure diseases which among others are incurable, to know what is to come and to foretell it." Later, in the Helgi Lays, the Norsemen refer to similar sibyls in Guernsey, and some connection may have existed or may have arisen between this cult and that of a primitive Cernunnos, with, in historic times, a confusion and perhaps a fusion of his followers with those of black Hecate herself.

I will add little here about the animal cults. In the Bronze Age the swan constantly occurs in connection with sun-worship, and there were cults of the ox and the horse. In the first Iron Age the chief beasts shown on the Hallstatt pots are the horse, which bore the Nords to victory, the swan, the ox, and the ram. In the next culture of La Têne we have the horse, the wild boar, the ox, the ram, and numerous amulets—amulets usually represent older beliefs—made in the form of the horse, the boar, the stag, and little naked men, which were worn by the women. The wild boar is most popular as a military device; and here I suspect an Alpine influence, since pork was by far the favourite food of the Lake-dwellers in Switzerland, who were not prejudiced like the Egyptians and other peoples of the Mediterranean; and perhaps had less cause to be, where pigs ranged oak forests instead of rubbish heaps, and were less likely to transmit *trichina* and other parasitic worms. Animal gods are mentioned, such as Moccus, a well-known swine god, and goddesses like Epona and Damona, who looked after horses and sheep; but these are best likened to the black-letter saints, by whom they were replaced; when in Brittany, for example, the pardon of St. Cornelly replaces the cult of the ox, whose interments and brazen images are found near by. Cæsar notes that the Britons did not eat the hare, the hen, or the goose (which probably includes not only the saviours of the Capitol and the martyrs of Michaelmas, but also our royal swan), though they kept them for 'amusement.' This means for religious purposes, since Boadicea, according to Dio Cassius, while exhorting her tribesmen to rise against the Romans, let loose a hare, and, when its course proved to be one of good omen, gave thanks to her goddess Andraste (whose name has a manly sound). A bear cult may also be traced in Deo Artio, and has left such names as Artigan and Arthgen, 'son of a bear'; d'Artagnan gasconading in the South; and Cormac Mac Art, suckled by a she-bear, who was more kindly than Elisha's helpful animals. Skin disguises were also worn by the Britons before they engaged in war and for some other ceremonies, as in the Lupercalia at Rome; while tales abound of half-human monsters slain by heroes, of men with the heads of cats and dogs and goats, and of the Leshi in the Northern woods with their goat legs and horns.

A final word may be said about the beliefs of the Northmen. Embodying as they did the Nordic concept of life, they were to influence the Northern churches so deeply that Dr. Carus declares that "Christianity to-day is essentially a Teutonic religion." But this is a partial and aristocratic view, for we have to reckon with the mentality of the Mediterranean Race, where a host of cults are included in a hierarchical system; a hierarchy which is 'infallible,' but is none the less open to all born dictators and is the aim of both Catholic and Fascist alike. We must also take into account the more abstract and communistic bias of the Alpine Race, which found its expression in a number of small congregational units controlled by a body of elders; a form which may also occur in any religion under persecution. All such conversions of Christianity to racial ways of thought and environmental needs will work upon this medley of heathen gods, and the Nordic Race did have a marked influence. We have, for example, the conformation of a solstitial year with midwinter and midsummer celebrations in the place of an older mode of reckoning, to which I shall refer later; while warlike gods or saints, Thor and St. Michael, will also affect the position of Cernunnos. But even in Scandinavia, where the Nordic Race was markedly dominant, behind Odin and Thor, Freya, Baldur and the evil spirit Loki with his mixed brood, the Fenris Wolf, the Midgard Orm and Hel, Queen of Nifelheim, whose name survives in Hell (under a male ruler)—behind all these we find stray references to Heimdal, an ancient god. Vigfusson and Powell have collected these from the sagas and eddas. "An ancient god is Heimdal, from whom the Amals spring. There are strange lost myths connected with him; his struggle with Loki for the Brisinga necklace; the fight in which they fought in the shape of seals. He is 'the gods' warder,' dwelling on the gods' path, the Rainbow. There he sits, 'the white god,' 'the wind-listening god,' whose ears are so sharp that he hears the grass grow in the fields and the wool on the sheep's backs, with his Blast-horn, whose trumpet-sound will ring through the nine worlds, for in the later legends he has some of the attributes of the Angel of the Last Trumpet. His teeth are of gold; hence he is 'stud-endowed.' Curious genealogical myths attach themselves to him. He is styled the son of nine mothers; and as Rig's father, or as Rig himself, the 'walking or wandering god,' he is the father of men and the sire of kings, and of eorls and ceorls and thralls alike." He is, then, father of all men, like Dis; his teeth and his struggle with Loki make him the guardian of treasure; in the oldest accounts, indeed, he sits—and Loki mocks him for sitting stupidly in the rain—at the entrance to the nether world. Rhys thinks that his blast-horn once grew upon his head, for in Norse poetry 'Heimdal's sword' is a curious term used for a man's head; and his older names of Heimdali and Hallinskidi are said to mean 'a ram.' 'White' is an unexpected epithet, but " in Welsh literature we find the king of the fairies and the huntsman who fetches the souls of the deceased named Gwyn, that is to say, White."

There is yet another Cernunnian strand. In that fine concept of Ragnarok, the Doomsday and the Twilight of the Gods—for doubtless these Nordic warriors could think of no better end than facing fearful odds—at the sound of the blast-horn Loki will lead, not only his own children, but an army of frost giants, against the Olympian citadel. In many legends these giants and trolls appear as the original owners of the land; they envy the newcomers and try to destroy their work; they come to collect some rent or sacrificial offering which is their due, they are slain by heroes who object to paying rent. We find amongst them the three-headed hoar-giant, Hrim-Grimnir of the Edda, who lives at the door of death. If the old horned god of the underworld had in part been given the post of warden to the younger gods, there is yet this giant Grim biding his time. Some also relate him to a triune god whom the Slavs knew as Triglaf.

As a comment, we can note that the lowest circle of Dante's inferno is an ice-hell—a Northern idea, since the men of the South favour hells of a volcanic nature—which is under the rule of Dis. As Carus says: " Dante's portraiture of the evil demon, whom he calls 'Dis' agrees exactly with the appearance of the principal Northern deity of evil. . . . Dis has three faces: one in front, and one on each side. The middle face is red, that on the right whitish-yellow, that on the left side black." As a matter of fact and not fable, when Pomerania was converted to Christianity in 1124, the threefold head of the Triglaf idol was broken off by Bishop Otto of Bamberg and was sent to Pope Honorius II. Krause suggests that Dante may have seen this triune 'Satan' when he visited Rome as the ambassador of Florence in 1301. This may have been so;

but Triglaf was not the only tricephalic god of the under-world.

If we turn back to the biological aspect of primitive magic and religion, we may with profit recognize that the main lines of such belief spring from three fundamental impulses, which can be found in every living creature: the impulse of Race-Maintenance and those of Self-Maintenance, which may, for my present purpose, be realized as the impulse to Feed, and the impulse towards Self-Preservation. More briefly, we can say that savages are driven by a desire to breed, to feed, and to avoid death. We have, then, in the magic of the hunters, rites which aimed at good hunting; rites which secured the fertility of the tribe; and burial rites which avoided the dire problem of personal extinction by assuring man of his survival after death. Paradoxical though it may sound, the cult of the dead may strengthen man's 'Will to Live' and powers of endurance. These are the three main strands which, like those of a whiplash, are plaited together, now one and now another strand lying uppermost in man's mind according to his need.

Even hunting tribes at the present day will, however, hold seasonal ceremonies to secure the increase of some special animal or fruit-bearing plant, and from these we have in neolithic cultures those fertility rites which centre around domestic animals and plants. The older hunting strand is, as it were, pinched out or overlaid by the fertility cults which now affect man's food, save in the wilder lands and amongst fishermen. But when man's control over his pastures, his fields, and his stored foods becomes more certain, the cult of the dead, in some races more than others, may expand to the dimensions that we can see in great necropoli, in the Pyramids, or in their Western equivalents, the dolmens and burial-mounds. Fertility rites, with the growth of accurate knowledge, may become a matter of rote; but death remains a mystery beyond control. In such cults, as I have tried to show, the old magician of the hunters rises again as the horned god, partly because of his unquestioned right over the caves, and partly because some warrior castes remain essentially hunters, though they have turned their arms against mankind. They hunt and they make war; they are ever exposed to sudden forms of death; their will to endure, their will to victory, must needs be strengthened by a firm belief in the after-life, where dreams come true. And these are not the dreams of the philosopher, or of the early Christian in his ecstasy, or of the Hebrew with his heaven of gold and precious stones; but rather an unseen world well stocked with game, with strong drink, and with women; a paradise with houris or a Valhalla where heroes may fight by day and feast by night. A world much like our own but with some obvious improvements, such as self-healing wounds, that will readily occur to the most simple soul. Even in ages of purer and vaguer desires, such a material concept will reappear when some great war or crisis shakes men's minds. Man's hope in a world to come will often vary inversely with his hopes in the world he knows.

But to continue. The concept of a Valhalla or an

Elysium with some contrasted domain of Hel or Tartarus has introduced that dual or twofold method by which for awhile men think. It is natural. We have, on the surface at least, our bisymmetrical bodies; our right and left, and our right and wrong. We live in a world of heat and cold, of night and day. The active hunters and warriors of the steppe and desert hunt and are bound by the day more strongly than those who trap by night or dwell in the greyer west. Light becomes set against darkness; like the Hottentots, they may see in the red of the dawn the blood of a conflict between the powers of light and darkness. In such a conflict there is both good and evil, god and the devil.

In primitive belief it may be said that the fear of evil, of famine, sterility, or utter death is greater and more powerful in its operation than a respect or a love for some beneficent power. In its vague form 'good luck' *may* be secured by various rites, but 'bad luck' *must* be warded off, and is the first to assume a more personal form, which must be propitiated or worshipped as a god. Nightmares are commoner or more impressive than pleasant dreams. Where positive observances are enjoined upon a tribe they are often of a prophylactic nature and are outweighed by negative commands. As in our nurseries, the words 'Don't' or 'Thou shalt not' rule the savage mind. The early gods are cast in a frightful form and have a minatory nature. But then comes the dualism in which so frequently the sun god conquers the power of darkness.

In the early days of war we can also see how the god of

a conquering folk, as their desire for conquest is increased, proceeds along the path which, in this material sense, leads to omnipotence. As the extended god of the Assyrians, as Jah, as Ormuz, as Allah, as the 'Old German God' of recent years, so he becomes the desirous warlord of his tribe. For a while he may be content to rule, *primus inter pares*, like Zeus or Odin; but sooner or later, when he gains supreme power or when his chosen seek an absolute conquest of new lands, the old indigenous gods, especially those so ancient and so rude that they can find no place in any pantheon, become identified with the devils and evil spirits of the new creed. At the same time, their priests and priestesses (so many of whom served the old gods of fear) are classed as wizards and as witches, warlocks and sorcerers, who serve the devil himself. The word 'magician,' which I have hitherto used in the simple sense of one who deals in magic, whether it be of the 'white' or the 'black' variety, may now have an evil meaning. None the less, I prefer to retain it as an ambiguous term, for though a conquering people or a triumphant creed may, for many good reasons, try to hunt out hostile and harmful warlocks, witches, and heretics in general, they may, none the less, traffic with more amenable magicians, with 'cunning men,' 'wise women,' and the like. Apart from purely psychical influences, such helpful aborigines may be most useful. Amongst a lot of rubbish they may have a knowledge of good herbs; 'Peruvian bark,' otherwise quinine, was a native remedy. Often they have an empirical and sound acquaintance with the local weather, with the wild animals, with supplies of water and ores beneath the ground. The helpful dwarf, the Lapland witches (who sold weather), water diviners, and crones with second sight are all familiar figures. Such knowledge, the skill which subservient individuals gain in reading character, in cunning, and in ambiguous prophecy—all these will often lead a conqueror to believe that his magic is weaker than that of the conquered race. The conqueror may respect his own gods, but he will consult those of the aborigines. Just as a man while admiring virtue in women will sometimes take advantage of its absence.

Exaggeration naturally creeps into all legends and mythologies. Larger aborigines are giants, titans, and trolls; for a discomfited Nord will not have been worsted by a puny foe. Aborigines smaller than the invading race become, in the course of time, pygmies and dwarfs and fairies. A native knowledge of the country, of secret caves and underground abodes, endows such beings with the gift of invisibility. Men dressed as animals become half animal or wholly so. A knowledge of poisons—the easiest means by which a subjugated race or sex can gain revenge—is a recurrent theme. The old magic by which the natives gained benefits for themselves—good hunting, fair weather, better crops, fertility of both man and beast— is now reversed against their enemies, so that they blast the wheat, raise tempests, and are the cause of impotence and infertility. Their own abode of the dead, indifferent though it may have been, becomes identified with a place of torment.

Similarly, some of the old and sacred animals may become malign; but here a large reservation must be made, for many may already have their place in the alien belief, and many are far too valuable to become taboo. Some lesser beasts may gain an evil repute; or, by a compromise, others may only be 'unlucky' in some particular connection. But most of them must be retained. So, also, much that is of practical value in the magic rites and many beliefs that are deeply engrained must be incorporated in the new faith and blended as far as possible with elements that are already present. Many old elements do not blend, but in an age that is uncritical or is free from the more exclusive forms of theological intolerance, they may still remain as curious patches in the pattern of some later religion despite their incongruity. In the more abstract religions such patches may be scarce, or a primitive framework may be concealed by a web of metaphysics and philosophy. In more material religions they may be conspicuous; they may obscure the essential doctrine, like the magical rites in Thibetan Buddhism or Taoist philosophy. Often in its ancient home one patch will stand out as some arresting local cult or 'heresy.'

But in all these mythologies, legends, and local cults; in fairy-tales and in superstitions; under much exaggeration and poetic fancy; under the usual rationalizations, fictitious explanations, and 'inventions' of layman and priest alike, there is a precipitate in which the old indigenous elements may still be found. In lonely places and in such a residuum the horned god still continues. Here and there details of dress, fixed dates for festivals, similar forms of magic in widely separated areas, similar names—though the philological method must be used with caution lest we " eat the insane root which takes the reason prisoner "—will reveal his presence and outline his form. It is often by reason of their trivial nature that such details have survived. Just as a zoologist can often distinguish one species from another, and, indeed, may only be able to do so by means of small but constant characters, such as the genital armature of a beetle or the arrangement of scales on a mosquito's head—by characters, in fact, which are not immediate adaptations to and therefore remain unchanged by the external environment of the beast—so likewise we must often depend upon trivial and vestigial details in seeking the historic descendants of the old magician. Similarly we must seek him in the byways of history, wherein the spirit of a people lives, rather than in the attested records of the political and ecclesiastical historians, who too readily dismiss the most potent legends and superstitions as baseless or unfounded, thereby imparting to their studies that aridity, dulness, and sense of unreality which has become proverbial. Some information may, however, be gleaned from the documentary evidence, and this bears witness not only to the real power which the magician holds over the mind of man, but to his continued existence in a tangible human form.

CHAPTER V

WITCH GOD AND DEVIL

The heathen West—The conversion of Christianity—Some early grafts
—The witch cult of the West—Walpurgis Nacht and Hallowe'en
—The Sabbath rites—Service and sacrifice.

FROM my remarks about the heathen religions of the
West it will be obvious that the early missionaries had
much to contend against. The Church might and did
obliterate Mithraism, whose rites bore such an embarrass-
ing resemblance to those of the Christians that Tertullian
was led to declare that "Satan imitates the sacraments of
God"; but this was also an Eastern creed. The war gods
of the fighting men, the sun cults, the fertility goddesses
of the farmers and peasants, and yet more primitive
elements, though also 'works of the devil,' were indigenous
beliefs, firmly rooted in the soil and in the minds of men.
Towards these the early Church often adopted an attitude
of toleration and transformation, before it could proceed
to that of persecution.

Some degree of toleration and compromise could be
extended towards pagan ceremonies which were of a harmless nature, like those of the mistletoe and the maypole,
as long as the participants stopped at the prelude, so to
say, and did not go too far. But since they usually did
go too far, the missionary Church adopted a policy of
transformation.

By transformation I refer to the process by which Christian observances were substituted for various native ceremonies; corresponding adaptations were made in the Christian calendar; and saints with a real or a fictitious character replaced the older deities and local gods. The most familiar examples of transformation will be found in any Church almanac, where the great events coincide approximately with the solar and lunar dates on which the more civilized pagans held their own festivities. Thus, the great Mithras sun-feast and that of Yule were hallowed by the Nativity of Christ; the summer solstice, with its Beltane fires, was marked by the Nativity of St. John the Baptist; and the vernal and autumnal equinoxes roughly coincide with Lady Day and Michaelmas. Easter moved with the Ostara festival of renewed growth, fertility, and the resurrection of life in Northern climes; for, as the Venerable Bede tells us, " the old festival was observed with the gladness of a new solemnity." This policy in regard to minor details also is clearly enjoined in a letter written in A.D. 601 by Pope Gregory to the Abbot Mellitus. The Pope's orders run that the ' *fana idolorum* ' are " not to be destroyed, but let the idols that are in them be destroyed, let holy water be made and sprinkled upon the said temples, let altars be erected and relics placed. And because they have been used to slaughter many oxen in sacrifice to devils, some solemnity must be exchanged for them on that account" (Bede). This was a wise and kindly policy, but elsewhere Bede regrets that one Redwald, King of the East Saxons, " in the same temple had an altar to sacrifice to Christ, and another smaller one to offer victims to devils."

Christianity, it is true, could present the eternal symbols of the communal feast, the mother and her child, the dying man; but it was difficult for the heathens to grasp their new significance, and they clung, as we shall see, tenaciously to their own modes of thought and their own forms of worship. The solemnities at first were little more to them than their own ceremonies that had been purged of their grosser details—and much of their pleasure and reality— and now received the sanction of the Church. The new saint continually became invested with the duties and attributes of some pagan god. When we read of the conversion of the West to Christianity, it is well to remember that the change was more apparent than real. It might even be truer to speak of the conversion of Christianity to the West.

For one thing, Christianity in the West was not a popular movement that began with the lower classes and then spread upwards. It usually began with the conversion of some petty king or chief who was moved by the eloquence of some courageous or tactful missionary, the insistence of his wife, or a desire to gain prestige. Even then these chiefs needed their war gods, and many of them bear a marked resemblance to Feng Yu-siang, that 'Christian' Chinese General, who has recently declared that he is 'an Old Testament Christian.' Or, if they did not find that Jehovah was a satisfactory substitute for Thor, worshipped St. Michael, who was lord of the heavenly host and therefore eligible, or a St. George, whose legendary history can hardly be supported by what is known of the two historic saints who bear that name. Even when a king like St. Olaf made his subjects choose without delay between baptism or death, it is doubtful if any real conversion was effected. Churches to the Virgin and other saints are built where the old temples stood, high places of sacrifice are given holy names, black-letter saints spring up at every village shrine and holy well; yet there are continual complaints that ancient magic is being worked and ancient ceremonies are taking place in an unaltered form.

Thus, in France and Spain we can cite the repeated prohibitions against heathen rites—often centring round some megalithic monument—that were pronounced by the Councils of Arles in 452, of Tours in 567, and of Nantes in 568. The first Council of Toledo in 681 continues to admonish " the worshippers of idols, those who venerate stones, who kindle torches, who celebrate the rites of springs or trees "; the second Council in 692 repeats this admonition. In the seventh century, in fact, many men in France and Spain, even those of the *civitates*, or cities, let alone the *pagani* and heath-men outside the more advanced areas, clung to their old beliefs and ancient cults.

For an early record in Britain I will cite the *Liber Pœnitentialis* of Archbishop Theodore (668-690). The thirty-seventh book of this treats " Of Idolatry and Sacrilege, and those who pay divine honours to certain Angels, and evil-doers, soothsayers, poisoners, charmers, diviners, and those who vow their vows otherwise than to Holy Church, and the man who on the Kalends of January goeth about in the masque of a stag or a bull-calf, as also of astrologers and those who by their craft raise storms." Penances are then ordained for those who sacrifice to demons, divine by birds, exercise the craft of a seer or charmer, make philtres, slay by spells, attempt to poison, procure abortion, cast lots; for a woman who divines or uses devilish evocations, who "hath placed her son or daughter upon the housetop or in the oven in order to ensure their health"; for anyone who burns wheat on a spot where a man has died to ensure prosperity; or "to ensure health to his young son hath passed the baby upwards through some cavity in the earth, and then hath closed fast the hole behind him with thorns and brambles; for anyone who has paid a vow at a clump of trees, at a spring, at certain rocks, or at a spot where boundaries meet, or at any other place whatsoever save in God's house, the church." May I say that one can find traces of all these practices—with the substitution of attic for housetop and the possible exception of wheat-burning—in England at the present day. Then comes the passage most relevant to my subject: "If anyone at the Kalends of January goes about as a stag or a bull; that is, making himself into a wild animal and dressing in the skin of a herd animal, and putting on the heads of beasts; those who in such wise transform themselves into the appearance of a wild animal, penance for three years because this is devilish." Summers has called attention to another reference by St. Aldhelm, of Malmesbury and Sherborne, to this practice in 685, and to some earlier records on the Continent. In the fifth century, St. Maximus of Turin exclaims : " What is it but frantic folly when men, created by God and in the image of God, transform themselves to herd animals or to wild beasts or to some monstrous shapes ?" St. Peter Chrysologus enjoins that Christians should strive to convert " all who have masqueraded in the likeness of animals, who have metamorphosed themselves as draught cattle, who have assumed the shape of herd animals, who have turned themselves into devils." In the sixth century, St. Cæsarius of Arles is as emphatic : " Is there any sensible man, who could ever believe that there are actually rational individuals willing to put on the appearance of a stag and transform themselves into wild beasts ? Some dress themselves in the skins of herd animals; others put on the heads of horned beasts; swelling and wildly exulting if only they can so completely metamorphose themselves into the animal kind that seem to have entirely abandoned the human shape." The Council of Auxerre in 578 (or 585) has a canon : " It is forbidden to masquerade as a bull-calf or stag on the first of January or to distribute devilish charms." Such practices seem almost universal in Britain, France, Spain, Italy, and parts of Germany, and they were denounced again and again.

But the Church was yet weak and they continued. If we turn back to England we find Egbert, Archbishop of York, in the eighth century denouncing " witchcraft." In the tenth century, " witchcraft and morth-work " (or murderwork, usually by spells) are prohibited in the laws of

Edward and Gunthrum, and of Athelstan; and in the ecclesiastical statutes of Edgar in 959, which forbid " well-worshippings, and necromancies, and divinations, and enchantments, and man-worshippings and the vain practices which are carried on with various spells, and with frith-splots, and with elders and with various other trees, and with stones, and with many various delusions, with which men do much of what they should not. . . . And we enjoin, that on feast days there be complete abstinence from heathen songs and devils' games." This enactment was repeated by Ethelred. In the eleventh century a law of Canute runs: " We earnestly forbid every heathenism; heathenism is that men worship idols "—it was, perhaps, advisable to be more explicit—" that is, they worship heathen gods, and the sun or moon, fire or rivers, water-wells or stones, or forest trees of any kind, or love witchcraft or promote morth-work in any wise."

We have in these documents alone sufficient evidence to show that, not only scattered superstitions, but very definite heathen cults still flourished in Christian times; and also that one cult in which men were disguised as certain horned animals has a wide distribution, which bears witness to its indigenous nature and to its great antiquity.

Another point which we may bear in mind is that, not only the laity, but the priests themselves were sometimes impregnated with the old beliefs, especially in wild or remote regions, like the Far West, where the Celtic Church was active for a while. There is, for example, the curious legend that a monk was buried alive under the first church at Iona, which, whether it is true or not, was told with pious approval, and is a clear tradition of the foundation sacrifices customary in many lands. Again, St. Boniface, who converted Upper Hessia, discovered on his return after a short absence in Rome that most of his flock had already relapsed into paganism, and many of his priests were equally ready to celebrate Mass or offer sacrifice to a heathen god. Even in later days the Church has sometimes recruited its priesthood hastily and in considerable numbers from men of the more backward classes who could no more free themselves from the native beliefs, with which they were saturated, than the recruits from the warlike castes could divest themselves of their aggressive traditions and arrogant mentality. In the seventeenth century infected priests are found conducting the Black Mass. For the moment I find a distinctly palæolithic flavour about the priest of Inverkeithing who, in 1282, was presented before his bishop for leading a fertility dance at Easter round the phallic figure of a god. He was allowed to retain his benefice.

Speaking generally it is clear that 'abominations' continued to flourish as of old amongst the folk of the hills, the forests, the fens, and the incult heaths, long after the Church had gained a firm foothold in the townships and the aid of the ruling classes. But, as the centuries passed, the policy of transformation bore fruit in the more civilized areas. The exotic shoots that the Christians brought from the East and grafted on various pagan stocks had taken hold. At least, the shoots that were not too alien to the

native stocks had done so. There were always some doctrines which could only be cultivated, and then with difficulty, in the artificial atmosphere of a monastery or a
hermitage; but others were thriving like roses on a briar.
Much of the vigour of the old gods and the old observances passed into the body of the Church, which thereby
gained an intimate contact with the lives of men and something of the elemental zest of the old magic which it has
not entirely lost. The names of the greater gods were
forgotten or lost their divine significance, though here
and there the names of some of the more obscure saints
may arouse our suspicions. The pagan ceremonies were
adapted and refined; the practice of human sacrifice, for
example, was discontinued, and witch-burnings, heresy
hunts, and the refinements of the Inquisition took its place.

In brief, the major religions of the pre-Christians gave
way to the ceremonies of the Church. But there was always
an intractable residuum with abominations which could
not be tolerated or transformed by the most catholic of
Churches. Nor was this merely a heterogeneous and discon-
nected mass of superstitions that had been rejected by the
Church. As the Church becomes stronger its attacks are
levelled more and more directly against one group of
practices and ceremonies which are usually stigmatized as
'witchcraft.' To return to my metaphor, the great trouble
did not arise so much from the fact that a pagan stock was
still sending up vigorous suckers from below the graft.
Such reversions could be disposed of within the Church
itself. We seem to be confronted with a specific and

entirely different kind of weed which called for extirpation, root and branch. This becomes more evident when the Church, backed by the secular arm, advances, no longer by outposts, but as an army of occupation, into the wildernesses of the West, drawing a line of great churches like fortresses around the fenland and planting its monasteries like blockhouses along the mountain ways. Directly the Church was strong enough—that is to say, tentatively in the twelfth, and more decisively in the thirteenth, centuries —it began a deliberate campaign against a definite heathen religion which was most 'devilish.' Nor can it be said— in a forlorn and pitiful attempt to justify the appalling horrors of the Holy Inquisition—that this religion was an alien weed, a shoot from the Gnostic heresy. As we shall see, it has all the marks of a native growth, deep-rooted in the wild heaths and the untutored hills. Sometimes there may have been slight attempts at compromise. There is a curious legend about St. Hubert. I find a St. Ceraunos, otherwise Cheron, and Charon was the ferryman of hell. This, perhaps, is a coincidence and these are minor details; for extirpation was the order of the day. It is in this witch cult that I recover the horned god and the magician.

I have paused over the policy of transformation since it has now removed, or has absorbed, the more dominant heathen religions. Where the horned god was once overlaid by a number of more or less tolerant cults, he is now opposed by one corporate body of belief. The old magician is stripped of later attributes. The keys of Cernunnos and Pluto pass into St. Peter's hands. The primitive figure that has endured in his ancient home is more starkly revealed by the fires of persecution. He is at bay, rebellious and unconquered. Sometimes, indeed, his cult increased when fresh devotees—the goats that are present in any human herd—sought respite from the

FIG. 4.—A DEVIL OF THE THIRTEENTH CENTURY.

From a manuscript of the Duc d'Anjou in the National Library of Paris. Here the devil has conventionalized horns and a horse's tail. In other medieval representations he is commonly given the horns of a goat, a bull, or a stag, and a long dragon's tail. (From Carus' *History of the Devil*. Open Court Publishing Co.)

sheep. While in the world of Christian thought, since he cannot enter in a friendly guise he appears as the adversary, the arch-enemy, and prince of the Western world (Fig. 4).

We are too apt to think that the witches and wizards who figure in history were merely crazed beldames or evilly disposed misanthropes that might crop up at random like any ordinary quacks or charlatans to exploit ignorance with charms and spells and secret remedies. At the present day this is mainly true, and in Britain, as far as I am aware—apart from clairvoyants, patent medicine mongers, palmists, and their like—only some fragments of what we may call *operative witchcraft* survive in certain families and coteries, like broken heirlooms from some fallen house. But the house from which these came was once a reality, and Miss Murray, in her most thorough work on *The Witch-cult in Western Europe*, has collected a mass of evidence, which proves the existence of a *ritual witch-craft* that embodied a definite religious belief. The evidence is mainly drawn from a large number of witch trials, and from these we discover that witches held the same ceremonies and the same beliefs in localities as far apart as Scotland and the Pyrenees. An objection may be made that much of this evidence was given under torture, but this does not account for many similarities, which even extend to minute details; and, moreover, this evidence agrees with some confessions that were voluntary. Another objection is that the ecclesiastical trials were often conducted in the same way, and that leading questions were put in order to secure a conviction. This regular procedure was, indeed, abused in some of the later witch hunts, but it may be more truly interpreted as a sign that the Church was well aware of the nature of the cult which it wished to destroy. Otherwise many of the questions seem to be quite childish. Inquiries about "fairies" are, for example, obscure until we realize that 'fairy,' 'elf,' etc., were used throughout Europe as bywords for members of the cult. For a convincing proof I must, however, refer the reader to Miss Murray's work. Here I shall take the liberty of quoting certain passages and of summarizing some of the essential features of the cult which Miss Murray has revealed.

She finds underlying the Christian religion "a cult practised by many classes of the community, chiefly, however, by the more ignorant of them in the less thickly inhabited parts of the country." It had well-defined rites, and a highly developed ritual. The organization was the same throughout Western Europe with but slight local differences, and the evidence bears out the statement of a New England persecutor that " the witches are organized like the Congregational Churches." The unit consisted of a small body of elders with a minister to conduct the services; the numbers of such a 'coven' or 'covey' in Britain being fixed at twelve witches—a witch might be male or female—and one officer (the unlucky thirteen). These covens would meet together on the great days under a chief who acted as god, and each "church" was an independent entity, though in the South of France we find a Grand Master who presided over several districts. The covens carried out various rites and experiments in magic, the *comptes rendus* being sometimes recorded in a book kept by the 'devil,' who also taught, and would, on occasion, reward or beat his followers.

The dates kept by the cult are particularly interesting, since they "suggest a pre-agricultural stage." The great festivals were held on May Eve (April 30), which was sometimes known as Roodmas in Britain and as Walpurgis Nacht in Germany, and November Eve (October 31), otherwise that 'night of power' called Hallowe'en. As a later addition, midway between these nights of power, we have Candlemas (February 2) and Lammas, otherwise the Gule of August (August 1). The original celebrations, therefore, belonged to the May-November year, "a division of time which follows neither the solstices nor the agricultural seasons; I have shown below that there is reason to believe that these festivals were connected with the breeding season of flocks and herds." To these were added the festivals of the "solstitial invaders," viz., Beltane at midsummer and Yule at midwinter; and also the movable festival at Easter; though the equinoxes were never observed in Britain. "On the advent of Christianity, the names of the festivals were changed, and the date of one—Roodmas—was slightly altered so as to fall on May 3, otherwise the dates were observed as before. Therefore, Boguet is justified in saying that the witches kept all the Christian festivals. But the Great Assemblies were always held on the four original days."

I will pause to comment upon this, for a glance at the calendar tells us that the Christians only attached minor saints, or rites of a somewhat vague nature, to these old dates. On the one hand the great events had already been attached to the solar year, and on the other the peculiar nature of some of the witch practices may have rendered the retention of such provocative dates inadvisable. I have been informed that, even at the present day, those waves of religious revival which sometimes sweep over our Celtic-speaking areas produce a marked rise in the illegitimate birthrate. As it was, the Church did occasionally allow masques in which men disguised themselves with horns and hides and tails, as in the medieval Feast of Fools or Feast of Asses wherewith some colleges and cathedrals were wont to welcome the New Year; but even on this date the results were often so lamentable that these feasts were continually being suppressed. Of the old dates, however, February 2 is the Feast of Purification (probably derived from the Februation ceremonies of Rome), the day of St. Laurence, and Candlemas, to which I shall refer later. April 30 was sometimes kept as Roodmas in memory of the Invention of the Holy Cross, and is the day of St. Catherine of Siena, St. Walpurga, and St. Erkonwald, "a prince of royal blood, son of Annas, a holy king of the East Angles." August 1 now counts as a lay holiday rather than the day of St. Peter ad Vincula, St. Ethelwold, St. Peregrinus, and the Seven Maccabees. But October 31, though it is marked by St. Wolfgang, St. Quentin, and three brother saints in Ireland, was so important to the Celts as their Samhain, or Feast of the Dead, that it could only be marked as Hallowe'en, the Eve of All Saints.

Many of the saints that I have mentioned are historic persons, but the legends about them are of considerable interest. To digress for a moment, there are also curious distributions of place-names, such as the hills named after

St. Catherine, St. Michael, and St. Ann (sometimes a corruption of Tane). One meets forlorn chapels to St. Leonard on heaths and lonely places; and 'Leonard,' in the "Pseudomonarchia Dæmonum" of Wierus, was one of the four great princes of hell, black master of the Sabbath and inspector-general of magic and sorcery. St. Hubert's conversion was effected, while he was hunting on Good Friday, by a miraculous stag which bore a crucifix or cross surrounded by rays of light between its horns. Thus he became the patron saint of hunters, with his feast day on November 3, and is said to have died on May 28, which is, by the way, the date on which St. Joan was burnt. So, also, one may suspect a connection between the legendary St. Hurlewin and a demon Hurlewayne, whom we shall meet later; or between Cernunnos and St. Ca... unos, *alias* Cheron. But here I can only commend these matters to any hagiologist who may care to crack the dry and brittle husk of historic fact.

Now I take up Miss Murray's account again. At a Great Assembly there were two gatherings. One was 'the Sabbath,' a public meeting of all the witches in the district, who feasted and danced and celebrated their rites, worshipped their god, and indulged in pleasurable orgies (Plate VI.). For, despite the jaundiced views of the Christians, the old witch cult was on the whole a joyous religion and their word Sabbath has no connection with the Jewish Sabbath, but can be most probably derived from the word *s'esbattre*, 'to frolic.' The other meeting, the 'Esbat,' which was not open to the public, was made up of those who directed the rites and ceremonies. It was a business council where the affairs of the cult were discussed by the officials, and the more esoteric rites, such as the preparation of wax images, candles, and the 'Flying Ointment,' were carried out by skilled hands. The meetings were held at fixed spots, sometimes near to water and often at some old standing stone or megalithic monument. Admission to the cult was voluntary, but it involved the renunciation (in faith if not in practice) of any other religion, vows of complete obedience, and initiation rites that, in the case of female witches, were of a painful nature. One might also be called upon to sign one's name in blood or receive a 'devil's mark,' which was sometimes tattooed in red or blue on the left shoulder and took the form of the foot of a toad or hare. The devil's marks sought for by expert witch finders were, however, usually anæsthetic spots or supernumerary nipples, which were supposed to nourish an imp—both natural phenomena of fairly frequent occurrence. In Brittany and in other regions, where we find hereditary 'fairy' families, the witches' children were dedicated to the god as soon as they were born, and thirteen was the customary age at which they were initiated into the cult.

Miss Murray considers the deity in his twofold aspect as a god and as a human being. As a god the deity became manifest and incarnate in the form of an animal, a man, or more rarely a woman. The first is the earlier form, since the god often wears the skin of some beast that was sacred to the tribe or was most used for food. When the

PLATE VI

THE SABBAT.

The witch god with a light on his brow and two companions are enthroned in the top right hand corner. Before them stands a child sacrifice or initiate. Elsewhere there are scenes of revelry; the collecting of toads, and the preparation of charms in a cauldron, the smoke from which enfolds the more fantastic concepts. (After a painting by Ziarnko. From Summers, *History of Witchcraft.* Kegan Paul & Co.)

[*fac*

god appeared in human form he was sometimes clad in red, but is most commonly a 'black man.' At the Great Sabbaths the god was disguised out of recognition, and the witches never admitted that he was merely a masker. The grim central figure was a veritable god to whom they addressed their prayers and adorations, to whom they dedicated their children, and for whom they would sometimes go willingly to the stake. A mass of evidence shows us that the god, with whom the witches had ceremonial intercourse, was not only masked but disguised in other ways. "The coldness of the devil's entire person, which is vouched for by several witches, suggests that the ritual disguise was not merely a mask over the face, but included a covering probably of leather or some other hard, cold substance over the whole body, and even the hands." The 'coldness' and 'scaliness' of which the witches often complain was due to the fact that a chief devil with a large following would be quite unequal to the demands that were made upon him, and would use adventitious aids to impress the celebrants. He is occasionally spoken of as an old man with a grey beard; and there was often a second devil, who was younger and more vigorous than his chief.

As a human being, the representative of the god might attend small meetings or visit his adherents in the ordinary dress of the period, making himself known by some password or token. Some of the great chiefs or Grand Masters have been identified with historical personages, such as Marshal Gilles de Rais (the "French Bluebeard") and the Abbé Guibourg, whose many crimes included the celebration of a Black Mass over the body of Madame de Montespan to enable her to retain and to monopolize the affections of Louis XIV.

The general rites were mainly concerned with fertility, and primarily with the propagation of human beings, in which case the celebrants were not necessarily disguised; and with the increase of animals, in which case they were: rather than the fertility of crops. There is, however, some mention of rain-making, and witches have always had the power of raising tempests. Dances took a very prominent place in the cult. The ceremonial dances were a complicated blend of follow-my-leader movements, in which the chief devil took the lead and, since no lagging was allowed, the second devil brought up the rear and 'took the hindmost' with a whip; together with ring dances that went widdershins (contrary to the sun) round a standing stone on which the 'black man' might be enthroned. Some of these dances survive, and one, known as "La Volta," is said to be the origin of the waltz. The feasts and dances often led up to ecstasies and orgies of a somewhat promiscuous kind; to the kind of 'sin' in fact that is particularly abhorrent to celibates and to persons of uneasy virtue; and is apt to lead to life rather than death.

The special rites included blood sacrifices, such as a cat, a dog, a hen, a red cock, or an unbaptized child, who might be offered up by its witch mother or stolen. The blood of the infant and distillations from its entrails and fat were used in the preparation of various charms. There is also evidence that the god might be sacrificed, sometimes in person and sometimes by a proxy in the shape of a volunteer or a criminal who was accorded the privileges of the god. In the tenth century a goat was sometimes used as a substitute. It is not definitely known how often the god was sacrificed for the benefit of his people—the numerous parallels that are to be found in Fraser's *Golden Bough* vary in periodicity—but sacrifices are believed to have taken place annually, triennially, and as more serious affairs at intervals of nine years. The ashes of the god were scattered over the celebrants to secure their fertility, or, according to the Christians, to blast their opponents' crops and herds and hope of posterity. Miss Murray holds that in the days of persecution recourse was had to the public executioner in order that the true nature of the rite should be masked, and that this explains why witches were always burnt and other mysterious occurrences.

Candles (or torches) also figure prominently in pre-Christian Candlemas festivals and were sometimes carried by the devil, as a true Lucifer, upon his head; while the phrase 'to hold a candle to the devil,' that is while he performed various rites, has become a common expression. Amongst some miscellaneous items we find wafers stamped with the devil's head and used in a 'blasphemous parody of the Mass,' and 'Flying Ointments.' The latter will serve to illustrate what one might call the reality of un-reality. Three formulas are known:

1. Parsley, water of aconite, poplar leaves, and soot.
2. Water parsnip (*Sium*), sweet flag, cinquefoil, deadly nightshade, bat's blood, and oil.

3. Water parsnip, juice of aconite, cinquefoil, deadly nightshade, baby's fat, and soot.

For parsley and water parsnip we may read hemlock and cowbane. A medical comment on this is that hemlock has little effect upon the consciousness but produces paralysis; that aconite produces irregularity of the heart's action, which in turn may cause the sensation of flying; and that deadly nightshade produces delirium, in which the celebrant, having absorbed attenuated doses of the three poisons through his or her skin, might well confuse a half-conscious dream with reality. Reginald Scot, in fact, describes how witches "rubbe all parts of their bodies exceedinglie till they looke red, and be verie hot, so as the pores may be opened, and their flesh soluble and loose." He also gives the account by Johannes Baptista Neapolitanus of an obliging and friendly witch, who, after thus anointing herself, fell into a most sound and heavy sleep: but when she awoke insisted that she had flown through the air. So other witches might be moved by dreams, as well as by reality, to aver that they had taken part in the joys of the Sabbath. Summers, however, notices that witches on trial very rarely claimed to have any real powers of levitation, though this recent writer himself believes in the actual existence of this phenomenon. Some, however, will prefer to regard the popular notion of a witch flying through the air on her broomstick as one that is based in part on these induced dreams and trances, which a witch might relate in a misleading form; and in part upon distant and frightened glimpses by noninitiates of the extraordinary leaping dances of the Sabbath, in which a broom or stick was sometimes ridden as a piece of symbolic ritual.

Miss Murray divides the witches' familiars or attendant imps into two classes: *divining familiars* in the form of an animal, usually a dog, which represented the devil; and *domestic familiars*, which are mainly reported from England and took the form of cats, weasels, toads, and mice; the smaller beasts being kept in pots or boxes. That any animal kept by a witch should be credited with supernatural powers is only to be expected. One has but to listen at the present day to our cat lovers and dog devotees. Miss Murray also lays stress on the limited range of the belief that witches could transform themselves into such animals as the witch hares and witch cats that are most frequent in Britain (with rarer transformations into dogs, mice, cows, and bees); or the goat in whose skin the French witches often sought to identify themselves with their goatish god.

There is also a strange preference for certain names. In the list that is given of the witches tried in Great Britain, we find that on adding the totals for cognate names, Joan, Jean, Jonet, and Jane come first with 107 unfortunates; then follow Bessie, Elizabeth, Elspeth, 78; Margaret, Margot, Meg, 71; Isobel, 40; Mary, 40; Katherine, Kate, 38; Ann, 35; Agnes, 31; Marion, 17; Alice, Alison, 17; Christine, 16; Helen, 15. There are nine Collettes, all collected from Guernsey, and seven Marjories, who should probably be included in the

Margaret group. Other names occur, but do not run into two figures. Miss Murray remarks on the fact that no Saxon names, such as Edith or Hilda, are found; that Alis-on and Mari-on *may* be connected with a British goddess, Anna; that Isobel is probably a Christianized pagan name, though she has no proof that it is a variant of Elizabeth. She offers no explanation for the predominance of Joan.

Sometimes a chief woman or queen of the witches is mentioned in the trials, but we have no clear information about this personage. "As a general rule the woman's position, when divine, is that of a familiar or substitute for the male god, though she may be retained as the 'Queen of the Fairies' or 'Queen of Elphin.' . . . But when the cult is recorded the worship of the male deity seems to have superseded that of the female." Here I venture to disagree, since I believe that this cult primarily centred round a male god, though he may sometimes have had a female associate. In an account given by a French inquisitor we read that in 1609 in the Basses-Pyrénées one could find "a queen of the Sabbath in each village, whom the devil had like a lawful wife." This particular "Reine du Sabat," therefore, would be little more than the devil's favourite.

This, of course, does not exclude the existence of some other cult, or the possibility that a female sometimes replaced or aided the male. Summers, in his most recent and learned treatise, cites two passages which are important, since they also provide us with early evidence that witches were organized and not merely a sporadic phenomenon. Thus, Johannes Gratian, in the tenth, or perhaps the eleventh, century, relates " that certain abandoned women turning aside to follow Satan, being seduced by the illusions and phantasms of demons, believe and openly profess that in the dead of night they ride upon certain beasts, with the pagan goddess Diana and a countless horde of women, and that in these silent hours they fly over vast tracts of country and obey her as their mistress, while in other nights they are summoned to pay her homage." Also John of Salisbury, who died in 1180, speaks of the popular belief in a witch queen named Herodias, who called together the sorcerers to meetings by night, when they had feasting, sacrificed babes to ghouls and ghosts, and gave themselves up to blasphemies and debauchery. There are many other allusions to this Herodias (who survives in folklore, but is no relation to Herod) and to Diana, or Habundia, and the women who followed her. But I must leave this goddess.

So much, then, for the existence and the bare form of this witch cult, which I will proceed to examine—it is at least permissible to do so—from a palæolithic point of view.

CHAPTER VI

THE EVOLVED MAGICIAN

The antiquity of witch practices—The May-November year—The
guise of a god—Candles and images—The Queen of Elphin—
The faery Joan of Arc—Basque Jannicot.

WE find, then, in the witch cult a central belief and certain
rites which are most primitive. The essence of this belief,
like the organization of the cult, may be found all the
world over where savages still work magic. We can see
in almost any land the ecstatic religious dance, which is
an excellent form of prayer. We still have homeopathic
and sympathetic magic when a savage drinks the blood
of his enemy and wears his teeth, or an Italian peasant
women is found on her knees in front of a dentist's show-
case under the impression that it is a potent reliquary;
when witches work upon wax images or we burn guys
and effigies. This world still sees the animal disguise and
the sacrifice of the god. The ceremonial use of red, which
is the colour of one's lifeblood, of fire, of flesh, and
pleasant fruits, has a stimulating effect on the mind of
any man : it is still preferred by children, nursemaids, and
simple-minded colonels; and is selected by many savage
tribes, although other bright colours may be more easily
obtained. All these are general features which take us
back to the hunting stage.

But there are some special details in the West which at least warrant a strong presumption that the witch cult and its devil are the lineal descendants of the Old Stone Age magic preserved in the Pyrenees. These details are, as I have warned the reader, of a slight and apparently trivial nature, but taken collectively, together with the dates of the festivals, the geographical nuclei of the cult, and the actual survival at the present day of racial types which agree with some of the Aurignacian races, they lead me to the conclusion that the old magician is the true ancestor of this witch god. If so, he reached his zenith in the thirteenth century, which Carus speaks of as "the devil's prime." For it was this same witch god that gave reality as well as an outward form to the popular conception of the devil that was an all-powerful obsession in the Middle Ages, and rose again in the turmoil of the Reformation. To a medieval mind, indeed, any untoward event—an earthquake, a storm, a cold in the head, or a disinclination to work—was directly due to the devil and all his imps. It was an age of faith.

First, let us take the four original dates on which the Sabbaths were held. Here we may say that if the ancient May-November year, which they mark, is "pre-agricultural," it is pre-pastoral as well. For recent archæological research has modified the simple view that mankind evolved progressively from a collecting and hunting stage, *via* the domestication of food animals to an agricultural stage. In some localities, for all we know, men *may* have domesticated animals before they cultivated plants, but, with the exception of the dog of the mesolithic hunters, we have no evidence that they did so. On the contrary, in the oldest civilized settlements that have been found, those of Susa in Mesopotamia and Anau in Turkestan, we find that though the earliest inhabitants cultivated grain, there is no clear evidence of the presence of domestic animals until later cultures, which are separated from the first by a considerable interval. Moreover, when civilized modes of life first enter Europe from the East, grain and domestic animals appear together in the earliest neolithic settlements of the Danube and the Swiss Lakes. Again, at the dawn of the neolithic period in the West, the site of Campigny gives us evidence of agriculture, imprints of barley on the pots and primitive milling stones, but no evidence of domestic animals. In the West, therefore, a pre-agricultural stage means at the latest the mesolithic or Middle Stone Age, and this, as I have said, differs in no essential features from the last phases of the Old Stone Age. For this and for other reasons I cannot wholly accept the suggestion that the witch festivals were primarily connected with " the breeding season of flocks and herds," if by this Miss Murray wishes to imply domestic flocks and herds. The central rites of the cult are especially connected with the fertility of man and with wild animals, such as the stag and the ox, which alone could represent the auroch and the bison, since both these animals were on the verge of extinction. If, therefore, we seek the origin of this year with a May-November summer and a November-May winter, we should probably look to the habits of the game and some periodicity in the lives of the ancient hunters themselves. These we can only surmise. But the Dutch names of Grasmaand for April and Slagtmaand, or "Slaughter Month," for November may carry some hint of the welcome that the old hunters would give to the new pasturage when the herds shift their ground and the migrants are on the move; and of the autumnal battue after the breeding season of many beasts. In the West, also, the springtime, and more particularly May morning, have ever been associated with thoughts of love; and we may remember that the Celts reckoned by nights and not by days (whence our 'fortnight' and 'sennight,' though the Celts used a nine-night week), so that Walpurgis Nacht would be the commencement of their year. So, also, Hallowe'en, which marks the end of their summer, is still the night on which maidens, by many charms, seek to find out the names of their future husbands. Midway between these two dates we have August 1, with the Lammas fairs and meetings and the Lugnassad fairs which were most important in ancient Ireland, where the old reckoning survived into historic times. Sir John Rhys, writing of the Lugnassad, says: "Marriages were solemnized on the auspicious occasion; no prince who failed to be present on the last day of the fair durst look forward to prosperity during the coming year. The Lugnassad was the great event of the summer year, which extended from the calends of May to the calends of winter. The Celtic year was more thermometric than astronomical, and the Lugnassad was, so to say, its summer solstice, whereas the longest day was, as far as I have been able to discover, of no special account. . . . Perhaps the marriages at Lugnassad followed a season of no marrying: in Scotland, at least, the month of May was a close time in this respect." There seems, therefore, a possibility that these dates marked a close season both for the men and for the beasts which they used to hunt. At present it is appropriate that the shooting season should end at Candlemas and that the Gule of August, the old British Gwyl or 'Feast,' should have been legally reinstated as Bank Holiday. But I must leave a more accurate explanation to those who are better versed than I in the old arts and customs of venery.

Without wishing to appear too plausible, I should like to compare the animal forms assumed by the witch god with the preference shown by the palæolithic artists for the wild horses (or the red deer) and then the bisons, goats, cattle, and reindeer. From the evidence given at the trials the devil most commonly appeared as a bull, a cat, a dog, a goat, and then more rarely as a horse or a stag. Sometimes the form was variable. At Auldearne, in 1602, he was reported as "a sterk, a bull, a deer, a rae, or a dowg"; at Alloa, "as a dog with a sowis head"; in Guernsey, though a cat guise was more usual, "in the form of a Dowg with two great horns sticking up"; at Windsor, "sometimes in the shape of an Ape and otherwise like a horse." A bear disguise occurs twice only, in Lancashire and Lorraine; but I suspect that "sowis head." A sheep form is mentioned in France, but this, as Miss Murray remarks, is possibly the goat. The goat incarnation was common in France; but it is not recorded from the British trials, though in our popular lore there is often a close connection between witches and that unhallowed animal. At Avignon, in 1581, the witch tells us that when the devil mounts a great stone to be worshipped " he instantly turnethe himselfe into the form of a great Blacke Goate, although in all other occasions he usethe to appear in the shape of a man." In the Puys du Dome he appears as a " great Blacke Goate with a candle between his horns." May we not be tempted to see some memory of the wild goats on the cave walls; of the dancing men in the skins of the chamois, that has now been replaced by the more common and most lustful animal; of the worshippers once led into the awesome caves by the old magician with a light fixed on his head, like our miners of the last century with candles in their caps. The bull, again, would succeed the vanishing bison and the wild cattle as a food animal and as a symbol of virility. Can the cat and the dog be derived from the larger carnivores, from the lions of clay and the ravening wolf? Some Devon witches did speak of the devil in the form of a lion; and the simile is a familiar one. A palæolithic carving of a cat was found in the cave at Teyjat; but this must represent the wild cat or the lynx, since our domestic strain was a late importation; and, indeed, hardly became common until the Middle Ages, if we may judge from the penalties imposed by the tenth-century laws of the Welsh prince, Howel

Dhu, on those who killed this animal. Soon, however, this prolific, nocturnal, and least domesticated beast became the favourite form taken by a familiar or by the witch herself. One might expect the deer to have been more commonly mentioned in the trials—it is only noted twice, once at Auldearne and once at Aberdeen—but we have the special prohibition by Archbishop Theodore of stag parties; the frequent medieval representations of the devil with the antlers; and some Cernunnian survivals that I must deal with separately. The rarity of the horse disguise is less curious, since the noble animal was so deeply involved in the religions and the chivalrous codes of the conquering race. Miss Murray calls attention to the fact that in Western Europe the pig is almost entirely absent from all the rites and ceremonies of the cult, as well as the disguises of the devil. I have already hinted at some reasons for this absence. The ass and the sheep are also missing; they have a prominent place in the Church. So, also, for that matter, does the lucky pig as the animal attendant upon St. Anthony of Padua and as a rival and alien symbol of fertility. These similarities between the preferences of the devil and the old artist may merely be due to convergence and coincidence, but the general resemblance is curious. So, also, is the fact that, though the god never did so, the witches (next to the cat, who may in part be a later substitute) preferred to change themselves into hares; the beast that the Britons did not eat and that is only represented once in the Old Stone Age (at Isturitz); but is then engraved on a loose piece of stone, like the Lourdes magician and the other portable works of art, nearly all of which have a definite magical significance.

I need not dwell upon the other palæolithic aspects of the cult. The use made of waxen images has its counterpart in the caves, and, as an instance of survival, Prof. Marett has recently referred to a waxen image of the village policeman that was found in Oxfordshire. The girl who made it, however, seems to have had only a vague tradition, since, though the image was transfixed with a hairpin, it was, I understand, the policeman's love, and not his death, that she wished to compass. The image and its heart should have been melted. The same authority accepts the interpretation that the palæolithic footprints in the caves, in which the toes are more deeply impressed than the heels, are those of dancers; and in addition to the waltz I shall have to mention some other dances that can more definitely be derived from a hunting phase. Then there is the great emphasis laid upon torches and candles. Torches, of course, were often borne in the Beltane and solar festivals, or lit from sacred fires and lamps tended by virgins, and will crop up in any religion. At the same time, the cave artists could only have worked by artificial light, and many archæologists have wondered how they could have painted so well by flaring torches or smoky Magdalenian lamps. Eskimo lamps, however, which are of the same simple form, need not smoke when they are carefully trimmed. The old artists have also left us crayons of fat and coloured earths moulded in horns or bones. Is it too much to suppose that they could also make candles of tallow or yet more smokeless ones of wax? In any case one must imagine that those who prepared the lights by which the magic artist could work, and by which the worshippers could grope their way into the secret caves, were highly skilled, and that in time their skill would become enshrined in ritual and superstitions, which did not change even when the ceremonies took place in the open. The candles that burn before our saints—which should, I understand, be of beeswax—may once have burnt before the sacred paintings in the caves. Thus one may link the honey bee with the sacred ox; and hazard a reason why, though they ignored a host of everyday occupations, the artists drew men gathering honey; why bees have become connected with witches and much super-stition; and for the widespread belief in the genesis of bees from dead oxen. The witch festival of February became Candlemas, a popular observance in pre-Reformation England, and much meaning was attached to the size of the candles, the way in which they burnt during the pro-cession, and their remains. An old translation from the Latin runs:

> "This done, each man his candle lights,
> Where chiefest seemeth he,
> Whose taper greatest may be seen;
> And fortunate to be,
> Whose candle burneth clear and bright:
> A wondrous force and might
> Doth in these candles lie, which if
> At any time they light,

THE EVOLVED MAGICIAN

> They sure believe that neither storm
> Nor tempest doth abide,
> Nor thunder in the skies be heard,
> Nor any devil's spide,
> Nor fearful sprites that walk by night,
> Nor hurts of frost or hail," etc.

The celebrants might have been going to the magician's studio. As it was, they were recalling Simeon's prophecy concerning "a light to lighten the Gentiles"; and at the same time securing a protection against the practices of the witches and against their god.

The palæolithic point of view that I set out in the first section may also help us a little in the problem of the 'chief woman' in the cult, which Miss Murray finds obscure. We should be inclined to say from this angle that the position of witches generally is that of participants who are strictly subordinated to the male magician, the position, in fact, of the women in any primitive community of active and warlike males. The chief often treated his coven with severity and would thrash them if they misbehaved. At times he had his favourite, who would thus gain precedence and lead the chorus, as the Cogul lady with the long plume may have done. But even if we allow for the power that an exceptional virago may gain, or the occurrence of female witch doctors amongst the Zulus, I doubt if it was usual for any female to gain high, permanent office. When she appears to do so, she would be, as Miss Murray believes, a substitute for the male god. Often a powerful ruler, who was not obsessed by a strong sense of duty, might object to being killed; and, apart from this, an old, wise chief might be too valuable for sacrifice in perilous times. This is often so in kindred cults, and in that case, when the periodic sacrifice is necessary, it does not so greatly matter whether the proxy god is male or female. One can then hardly speak of the supersession of a female god.

But there may be another source of confusion in that vague "Queen of the Fairies," "Queen of Elphin," Diana, Hecate, Herodias. In some of these there may be a trace of the Aurignacian goddess, but whatever her worship may have been, it seems to have had little connection with the rites in which slim Cogul women dance round a male, or witches ride abroad. The Aurignacian idols would not dance well; and, moreover, a benignant cult of expectancy had probably been absorbed into those of the pregnant Cybele and various Christian saints. More probably, as I have suggested, this Diana of the West represents some virile goddess. There may be a tribal and geographical coincidence of the male and female cults, which, under persecution, might amalgamate against a common foe. Yet I doubt if the magician and the Aurignacian goddess, and still less the witch god and Herodias, were really on friendly or intimate terms. Even our Oberon and Titania had their differences about the adoption of a child, which again might be due to some prior reluctance on Titania's part.

It is not entirely relevant to my subject, but I refer the reader to Miss Murray's interesting thesis that Joan of Arc was a female proxy, gentle, perhaps (like Florence

Nightingale!), but none the less a fanatic in her faith, as many witches were. Anatole France has seen in Joan the rallying point of a great and powerful organization that was opposed to the Church party. Miss Murray identifies this with the witch organization that permeated the lower classes in France and England, and had also many adherents amongst the nobles and clergy. If Joan was looked upon as an incarnation of the god, this would explain the enthusiasm and confidence which she inspired, and if as such she was foredoomed to sacrifice, it would explain why, as the fatal day approached, the French never lifted a finger to ransom or to rescue her. A few instances can be cited, and more may be inferred, where witches had recourse to the public executioner to disguise the real nature of the rite. From this point of view the trial would be a test match between the old religion and the new; and the questions put to Joan concerning 'the tree of the Faery ladies,' at which she received her mission, become significant. The 'Voices' and 'St. Michael' and 'St. Katherine' became pseudonyms; and her refusal to describe 'St. Michael' ("I saw him as well as I saw you." ... "My king and many others have also seen and heard the voices") is easily understood. The judges made a great point that her retention of male attire was a sign of the Dianic cult. She first heard the voices at the initiation age of thirteen. In brief, "the conduct of her associates during her military career, as well as the evidence at her trial, bear out the fact that she belonged to the ancient religion, not to the Christian. Nine years after her death in the flames, her commander, Gilles de Rais, was tried on the same charge, and condemned. . . . Like Joan herself, Gilles received semi-canonization after death, and his shrine was much visited by nursing mothers." This thesis may not find favour, especially in view of St. Joan's recent canonization and her position as a focal point for many finely wrought ideals. The evidence against Gilles de Rais is, however, conclusive, and he was closely associated with Joan, though he made no attempt to rescue her. He came of a Breton faery family; he is known to have sacrificed about 150 women and children in the witch rites and, according to popular tradition, for his researches into alchemy. His execution took place at the sacrificial interval of nine years after the death of Joan.

Before we leave the trials we can note that in the Basses-Pyrénées the evidence "makes it clear that a disguise was worn and that the mask was placed on the back either of the head or the person"; or in one instance "le diable estoit en forme de bouc ayant une queue, et au-dessous un visage d'homme noir." Without entering into many curious representations of the devil and some common expressions that may be a legacy from this form of disguise, I must recall the two-faced Janus. Two names for the god are also recorded. One is "Hou," which appears in Breton place-names and in the summons of the Guernsey witches, "Har, har, Hou, Hou, danse ici"; the other is Jannicot, which is found in the Pyrenean incantations, "In nomine Patrica, Aragueaco Petrica, Gastellaco Ianicot, Equidæ ipordian pot"; "au nom de Patrique, petrique d'Arragon. Iannicot de Castille faictes moy vn baiser au derrière." Jannicot was an old Basque god. There may then be a possibility that he is related to the ancient Janus or Dianus, and either form would account for the predominance of Joan as a witch name. The Basque superstitions and the singular language, which according to a temperate authority comes midway between certain American and some of the Ural-Altaic tongues, might shed much light upon our subject. The Basque word for the deity, "Jaincoa" and "Jaungoikokoa" (said to be the origin of our 'By Jingo'), is little more than 'Jaun,' meaning a 'lord' or any master of a house, and probably 'Goikoa,' the moon, but it is curious to note that their word 'Akhelarre' for the Sabbat has still the literal meaning of 'the goat pasture.' There are also many tales about the Basa-Jaunis, who was a wild man, a wood sprite, and a satyr, and the Basa-Andre, who was a wild woman before she became a witch or sorceress. The Basques also have preserved specimens of almost every kind of dance, including animal dances, in which men personate such beasts as the bear, the fox, the horse, etc. I cannot, however, dive deeply into what may well be a pool of palæolithic survivals. We have yet to seek the magician as the horned god of the dead, and here I will leave the courts and turn to folklore.

CHAPTER VII

HERNE AND HIS KIN

The fact of magic—Glamour and witchery—Herlechin and the priest —Wild huntsmen and phantom troops—Herne with great ragg'd horns—The Mongol Erlik-khan.

WE can now see that from the dawn of our history and on into the fifteenth century there was a powerful and widely spread religion which had survived from very early days; and at times even gained ground as a reaction against the more repressive and inhumane forms of Christianity. We must, therefore, be prepared to give some credence to certain popular tales, which, though adorned by their tellers, none the less had, or could have had, their basis in solid fact. So also, if we know anything at all about the power of suggestion and counter-suggestion, we must admit the truth of many 'vain superstitions.' The imaginative or magical interpretation of a phenomenon may be wrong, but the reality is there. The witches believed in the divinity of their incarnate god: the Christians believed in the devil that walked abroad, fearsome and horned, or as an ordinary man. Both credited the devil with attributes, which we may doubt; but he had disguises and powers which did exist in a material form, and sent out emissaries (like the agents of Gilles de Rais). To use a simile: Pink rats may be the product of

124

delirium; but real rats do exist; and can be dyed for thaumaturgic purposes.

Let us remember that on certain nights a belated Christian—like Tam o' Shanter—might, apart from any hallucination, have stumbled upon the black horned figure and the warlocks and witches at their devilry. And such an intruder, especially in the ages of persecution, would be in real and imminent peril as a suspected spy. Babes were stolen and sacrificed in unholy ways. Poisons, both mental and physical, were employed against the enemies of the cult by magicians and malignant hags. Men could and did sign covenants with the devil in their own blood. There is no reason why this devil should not be included in the ancestry of many a noble family, as in the legend of the Angevins. Conversely, a wandering knight might easily be charmed by a fair young witch, no bungling amateur in her seductive craft. The shallow materialist may dismiss the trials of early saints that fled to the wilderness. Some diabolical forms or the temptations of a St. Anthony can be recognized as familiar dreams: the nemesis of those who seek to free themselves from the temptation of the flesh and so become the slaves of a strong obsession. Yet when the rustic mind still takes such a pleasure in tormenting the stranger or the defenceless man, it is too much to suppose that the wizard and his followers would leave a saint alone. Saint-baiting must have been a favourite sport; and an irascible hermit would be a godsend to the heathen villagers. The local devil would be most personal. The witch cult had its horrible side, the 'bad magician' and the 'wicked fairy,' the usual dominant hags and lecherous old men. Churchmen, to deter their flock, would emphasize this and paint the devil as the black lord of hell. But though our early records are almost entirely written from the monastic point of view, the attractive and joyous side of the old cult sometimes shines through. And yet more beautiful derivatives may be found in oral traditions of fairy folk and in old tales of the fair Tiphaine and Melusine, 'Madge Grey' and 'Cutty Sark'; and in our common use of words like witchery, enchantment, glamour, charm.

The popular conception of the devil, in fact, with horns and hoofs and a tail, holding high revelry at night by pagan stones and hills, and rites that were riddled through with joy and fear, owes much of its form and substance and reality to this strong cult. But the devil of the priests —apart from the theological aspect, which I do not wish to discuss—also embodied many Eastern beliefs, together with attributes taken from other gods. His hell becomes a limbo of dying creeds. Thus Carus in his *History of the Devil*, remarks that "in the thirteenth century the devil reached the acme of his influence, and it is only possible to give a meagre sketch of the devil's activity during this period. Nothing extraordinary could happen without it being attributed to him, and to the people of the Middle Ages many things ordinary to us were very extraordinary." The old magician, I would say, shares in this apotheosis, but for the moment I turn back to another strand which will best serve to illustrate continuance and

PLATE VII

THE DEVIL ON THE STAGE.

A late appearance of the devil in his ancient guise as a stage character. The title page of an English masque presented in 1620. (From Summers, *History of Witchcraft*. Kegan Paul & Co.)

to recall Cernunnos, god of the dead, before his office was so unequally divided between St. Peter and Satan. This is an old superstition, and for my text I take the oldest record that is given, with much detail, by Ordericus Vitalis in his *Historia Ecclesiastica*. And thus the story runs:

At the beginning of January in the year 1091, a certain priest, named Guachelmus, of the village of Bonavallis, in the diocese of Lisieux, went out one night to visit a sick man who lived at the farthest end of his parish. On his way back, while he was still a long way from any human habitation, he heard a noise as of a great army approaching. In his terror he was about to hide himself behind some trees when the moon shone out and revealed a gigantic personage, who, raising a huge club, ordered the priest to halt and not move a step farther. The priest obeyed, and past him came an immense crowd of wailing ghosts, consisting of women and soldiers and ecclesiastics, amongst whom he recognized many of his own neighbours who had died recently. When these spirits had passed by, the priest said to himself: "It is no doubt Herlechin's troop (*familia Herlechini*). I have heard say that many have seen it formerly; but I rejected the report with incredulity and ridiculed it. . . . But now I have really seen the shades of the dead." Ordericus says: "This account I heard from the mouth of the priest himself."

We may allow for a pardonable degree of exaggeration, sceptic though this priest seems to have been. The sudden form which brandished a club over his head may well have appeared gigantic in the uncertain moonlight. It is very natural for the human mind to believe that it recognizes familiar faces in strange apparitions. We have all suffered from good ladies who find likenesses to those they know in cloud forms, gnarled trees, and ancient photographs. In jest—when in an age of faith the tale would have passed as truth—we hear of the soldier who was so close to the 'angels of Mons' that he recognized his aunt. According to a local tradition, Guachelmus met the troop at the cross-roads of Fosses-Malades, where many were buried who had died of the plague. This may have influenced his mind. One may also wonder if in troublous times witch devotees, as smugglers and poachers have done, donned the attire of dead relatives to scare away intrusive folk.

But there is this reference to a well-known superstition of Herlechin and his ghostly troop, and an anonymous writer in the *Quarterly Review* for October, 1902, has gone deeply into this piece of lore. He does not speak of the witch cult or prehistoric times, but in his "Evolution of Harlequin" the reader may find some points which bear upon my theme.

First take the word itself. "In old French writers it is found running almost through the gamut of letter changes, as 'herlequin,' 'herlekin,' 'hierlekin,' 'hellequin,' and 'hellekin,' being used as the name of one of those numerous hobgoblins which tormented the peasantry of medieval Europe with nameless fears. In the *Miracle de St. Eloi* (p. 110) it seems to be employed as a synonym for

Satan himself in the phrase 'par le consel de Herlaken'; and it is said to survive still in the folklore of provincial France as a name for the *feu follet* or will-o'-the-wisp. Indeed, our own Dorset folk use 'harlican' as an abusive term for a troublesome imp or youngster." I like to think of them still doing so, where we find, cut in the chalk above the village of Cerne Abbas, that giant, markedly ithyphallic and brandishing his club, to whom, so tradition tells, women once went by night with results that might have been obtained by the Sabbat rites or those of the Cogul cave.

But to return to the word. "In Old French poems and legends it is appropriated to a grisly being who was regarded as the personified leader of the phantoms of the dead. 'La maisnie Hierlekin,' or 'la maisnie Helequin,' is a phrase frequently used by French writers of the thirteenth century to denote a troop of ghosts or evil spirits which were believed to ride abroad at night, like the Wild Huntsman and his cavalcade, and were sometimes seen to engage as combatants in the air. . . . Indeed, the 'Hellequins' or 'Herlequins' of French folklore still disturb the forests of Jura and Franche-Comté with their fantastic hunting as they ride upon the winds. M. Le Prévost notes that the host seen by the priest must have been 'the Hunt of Hennequin' (otherwise 'la mesnie Hellequin'), who is still known in country parts as a great hunter, who, having sold himself to the devil, is compelled to return to earth during the storms of night which occur in Advent, attended by his huntsmen and dogs.

"In some districts of France and Germany folk-etymology has played around 'hellequin' and transformed the word into 'allequinti' and 'Caroloquinti' (in Hesse 'Karlequinte'), and then invented an ætiological legend that the spectral horsemen which form his troop are the ghosts of the army of 'Charle-quint' or 'le quint Charles.' Thus the old French *Chronique des Ducs de Normandie* (twelfth century) asserts that 'la mesgnie Hennequin,' which on one occasion appeared to Duke Richard the Fearless, accompanied by strange noises, was nothing else but 'la mesgnie Charles-Quint,' 'who was formerly King of France'; and a passage in the *MS. du Roi*, quoted by Le Roux de Lincy, similarly identifies 'Helquin' with 'Charlequin,' and his retinue with 'la gent au Charle-quint.'"

I have quoted these old French conversions, of an unintelligible word into the name of a fictitious king, in detail to prepare the reader for some similar explanatory efforts; and for the common way in which an intelligible name or even that of some historic personage is commonly substituted for a strange word or half-forgotten shade. And this superstition has a wide range. William of Paris, who died in 1240, refers to the "nocturnal horsemen who, in the French vernacular, are called 'Hellequin' and in the Spanish 'the ancient army.'" The apparitions were, therefore, well known in the region where the witch cult was most powerful. But in Teutonic lands, though in Holland we still find 'Hellekin' as a ghostly wild hunter, we get another rendering of the word in which the ending 'kin' is used for 'tribe' and the prefix 'hel' stands for the underworld of ghosts and demons, once ruled by the goddess Hela. The leader and his host become confused. The latter stand out in the Anglo-Saxon 'helle-cynn' and 'heoloth-cynn' used in the *Book of Exeter* for the ghosts or demons of the underworld. So we pass on to the old English superstition of the Herlething, Herle's company, or the Heleth-kin, a phantom host described by Walter Mapes, who became Archdeacon of Oxford in 1197: "The night-wandering troops which were called Herle-things appeared down to the time of our Sovereign lord Henry 2, a host which, strangely silent, circled round madly and wandered endlessly, among which were observed many who were known to be dead." This host, he says, was last seen on the borders of Wales and Hereford in 1154. Now, just as the French chroniclers found Charles the Fifth in harlequin, so Mapes, taking 'thing' in the sense of 'an assembly,' devotes a chapter (*De Herla Rege*) to a mythical Herla, 'a very ancient king of the Britons.' The writer in the *Quarterly Review* continues: "This very shadowy king Herla, according to another tradition, had been drawn by enchantments into a mountain cavern at the wedding of the king of the pygmies, and, after remaining a long time unconscious, had returned only to find that Saxon invaders had taken possession of his kingdom during his absence; so that ever afterwards he wandered at large, a discrowned monarch and a homeless vagrant. We would suggest that in this mythical wanderer Herla we may probably see the prototype and original of another kindred being, not less mysterious, who has proved a complete puzzle to folklorists, Shakespeare's Herne the Hunter, who is introduced in the *Merry Wives of Windsor* (Act iv., Sc. 4) as well known in ancient tradition:

> "There is an old tale goes, that Herne the hunter,
> Some time a keeper here in Windsor forest,
> Doth all the wintertime, at still midnight,
> Walk round about an oak, with great ragg'd horns;
> And there he blasts the tree, and takes the cattle,
> And makes milch-kine yield blood, and shakes a chain
> In a most hideous and dreadful manner.
> You've heard of such a spirit; and well you know
> The superstitious idle-headed eld
> Received, and did deliver to our age,
> This tale of Herne the hunter for the truth."

This hunter of the night, who is also a malicious spirit, cannot be separated from the 'Grand Veneur de Fontainebleau,' and is of the same lineage as the Hel-huntsman who led on the chase of the 'mesnie Hellequin.'"

Two conclusions are drawn by our anonymous author. The first is that "Whatever the ultimate origin of the name, Herlekin, when he first emerges into European folklore at the close of the eleventh century, was evidently a personification of death, or the world of the dead, whose shadowy crew he headed in their flight." And, secondly, "it has no doubt already occurred to the reader that the phantom host of Hellekin (or Herlekin), which we have met under various forms, is only another phase of the weird superstition of the wild hunt, the rout of restless, wandering spirits, which were so widely diffused all over Europe."

As the Latin *cornu* changes into *horn*, so *Cerne* might change to *Herne*. In any case, the reader may also be prepared to recognize Cernunnos and the older magician, who now emerge as the Wild Huntsman. My assumption that these two forms have been derived from the same palæolithic ancestor and can, indeed, be regarded as two aspects of one central figure, will help us to understand the identification of Herlechin and Herne, whom I will take as the most familiar example of the huntsman. Their persistence and the circumstantial accounts found in some of the chroniclers were, I would say, strengthened by actual encounters with chiefs of the witch cult. The old tales are, of course, loaded with many inventions. The rout flies through the air; here the chronicler would be infected by the popular misconception of the witches' power. Combats in the air are 'seen by many'; here we must allow for the forces of mob psychology and the well-attested phenomena of mass hallucination. In this light even the explanatory legends of the fabulists and the terms which they use may contain more truth than these historians suspected. William of Paris may well speak of the 'ancient army' in Spain—ancient, that is, by about 9,000 years. The hunter who sells himself to the devil and then must join his nocturnal rout, may stand for a convert to the old religion. Even the mythical King Herla was enchanted by secret rites held in a cave by the chief of some 'pygmy' aborigines, and then returns, as the witch god did, when the full force of the last Nordic invasion was spent, to continue as a vagabond in his ancient realm.

These old wives' tales, in fact, like the stray wandering lines in a puzzle-picture of "Find the White Cat" (the 'cat' is a patch of sky surrounded by the branches of ancient trees), at first confuse our view, but then fall into place to outline the old magician, Cernunnos, Jannicot. Then, as Christianity spreads to the wildest lands, Cernunnos, otherwise Herlechin, as god of the dead, becomes more definitely merged into some devil in the Christian Purgatory, and the magic huntsman stands clear again as Herne, that apparition of a dead keeper to Christian folk, the Windsor witch god to his devotees. And we have not only Falstaff "disguised like Herne with great horns on his head" (which he offers, by the way, to present to the husbands of the merry wives), but also the children disguised

"Like urchins, ouphes, and fairies, green and white,
With rounds of waxen tapers on their heads."

"They are fairies; he that speaks to them shall die," says Falstaff. Once it was doubtless unwise to meddle with 'fairies' or to call them by their true name. This superstition is still common in the more conservative parts of Ireland. It is also pleasant to read that "legend has been busy recently with the name of 'Herne the Hunter' at Windsor. His ghost is alleged to have been seen riding through the Home Park, and his horn has been heard more than once in the night stillness" (the *Morning Post*, November 3, 1926). I must now conclude this chapter on the wild huntsman with two very curious divagations from the same authority in the *Quarterly Review*, though I interpret them in a somewhat different way.

Following a philological trail, we may take the form *herl* or *erl*. There are, of course, plenty of genuinely wicked earls in history; but there is a strong suspicion that some of them have also been saddled with the bad character of the evil spirit. So also we have tales of 'Hurlewayne's meynie,' a disorderly rout of vagabonds; and the list of 'bugs' or devils in *The History of Witchcraft*, by Reginald Scot, includes 'the Hellwain, the Firedrake, the Puckle,' etc. Incidentally, the Fire-drake may have helped in the late identification of Sir Francis Drake with the wild huntsman on Dartmoor; and the Puckle (besides being a disease of cattle) is our friend Puck, an emasculate version of the medieval pouke, who was commonly identified with the devil, but goes back to the pooka, or, in Irish, *phooca*, and who, as Yeats rightly says, was "essentially an animal spirit."

But our author makes another cast, and so we find, like the British King Herla, an old Danish ellerkonge, who was popularly supposed to be the elver-konge, king of the elf-folk. Herder the poet altered this word when he translated the ballad of "King Olaf and the Erl-king's daughter"; Goethe made it famous as the Erl-konig. Behind it in Europe there stands ever the concept of the king of the dead. And now the philologists and the folklorists are in full cry, for three of them at least have identified the erl-konig with the Mongolian 'Irlechan' (Taylor), otherwise Erlik-khan. In a Kalmuk folk-tale a young khan or lord goes, like Orpheus, to seek his wife in the realm of Erlik-khan, "a black fortress surrounded by a moat of human blood and surmounted with a banner of human skin—a description which recalls the forbidding aspect of Hel's stronghold in the Edda. The two guards of this ghastly building are the 'Erliks' or servants of the Erlik-khan. . . . This Kalmuk Pluto, as king of the lower legions, wears a terrific appearance, his head being crowned with dead men's skulls and surrounded with flames." This Kalmuk tale comes from Central Asia, and in Thibetan art their Aerlik-khan is depicted as a masked figure with lofty horns, brandishing a club or a mace carved into a skeleton at the top. There is a further identification of this divinity with the Indian Yama of the Rig-Veda, who was lord of the dead and then became an equally diabolic ruler of hell. But I feel that we have gone far enough. Now my author inclines to the opinion that the erlik-khan is the precursor of the erl-konig myth in its later form and of the word 'erlechin,' which is, he says, not an Aryan word, and, therefore, may have been borrowed from Mongolian peoples such as the Lapps, the Ugrian Finns, and the hated Tartars; like other words that have an unpleasant meaning—e.g., Hune (i.e., a Hun), which is used for a giant, Taterman, in German a goblin, Tartarus, Ogre, etc. This may be so as regards the word. But I would say that the movement of a label, though it may serve as a clue, does not provide any proof that the myth itself is derived

from Thibet, and still less from India. There is more to
be said for the assumption that the belief was indigenous
to Europe, though similar and parallel growths from the
palæolithic stock may, of course, have evolved elsewhere.
In any case, it is interesting to find a horned and masked
and ring-straked god of the underworld at the end of our
philological chain in far Thibet. This form, then, may be
taken as an instance of convergence; while the similarity
of 'herlechin' and 'erlik-khan' may be a curious coincidence, followed by a confusion and an assimilation of the
two words when the Mongolians came into the West.
There was a similar confusion when Raleigh took the
American-Indian word 'Hu-rakan,' a storm devil, and
instead of adopting it as 'hurricane,' spelt it as 'hurle-
cane.' Or, though I shrink from the suggestion, is it
possible that Erlik-khan, as well as Cernunnos, sprang
from the Magdalenian magician? Certainly the Magdalenian culture has been found in Siberia; there is a strong
belief that it extended across all Asia; Sollas sees in the
Eskimos the direct descendants of these people. Is Erlik
an older word than we suspect, with its Tartar meaning
of *er*, a man, and *erlik*, strength and virility—a suitable
name for the dominant aspect of the old witch god?

Lastly, another stream comes in with the Italian
alichino, who, like Dis, is found as one of the ten demons
in the *bolgia* of Dante's *Inferno*. This changed to *arlechino*, and so passed on to the Western stage as our
familiar harlequin. But this is an incident in the decline
and fall of the ancient god.

CHAPTER VIII

THE DECLINE OF THE DEVIL

The stake and the inquisition—Witches and Manichees—The harvest of hate—Counter-magic—Relics and dead men's bones—The Black Mass, the 'Goats,' voodoo—The death of the devil.

THE decline of the horned god may be considered as the result of four processes—that of transformation, by which the Christians gave him an important post in their own Purgatory; that of persecution, by which they endeavoured to extirpate his worshippers; and that of ridicule, which is ever a potent weapon against the mystery-monger. Lastly, there came the growth of science which enabled intelligent men to detect many impostures and to produce by natural agencies many of the results that were formerly ascribed to the supernatural arts of the magician.

Little more need be said about transformation from an ecclesiastical point of view, for the Churches of the West became sufficiently powerful to substitute force for conversion, and at the same time the witch cult devotees, embittered by persecution, became more and more antagonistic and irreconcilable, even indulging in deliberate parodies of Christian rites, which rendered any attempt at compromise impossible.

The process of persecution, however, reveals many interesting facts, though the story is one that can only

138

attract the sadist or the theologian. As soon as the Church was strong enough, the earlier denunciations of the various councils were embodied in Papal Bulls, which, though they speak in general terms of 'heresy,' were, in Western Europe, directly aimed against the witch cult and against its palæolithic strongholds round Toulouse. This point is apt to be obscured by the Manichean heresy, which, originating in the East, did reach Europe about A.D. 1000; is said to have gained some ground during the eleventh century; and is generally believed to have given rise to such sects as the Bogomiles, Waldenses, Patarini, Cathari, and the Albigenses. But, as Dr. F. G. Buskitt, an authority on this subject, says, "I think it misleading to call these sects, even the Albigenses, by the name of Manichees." The localization of these cults in the wilder and poorer areas, their tenacity and endurance, the evidence given at the trials, all lead to the conclusion that the bulk of their adherents, in Western Europe at all events, were merely witch devotees under a different name. Carus remarks that "the witch-persecution mania was a general and common disease of the age," and that "it was natural that heretics should always be regarded as belonging to the same category as witches and wizards, for they, too, were, according to the logic of ecclesiastical reasoning, 'worshippers of Satan.'" This medieval point of view is still maintained in a recent work on *Witchcraft and Demonology*, by M. Summers. Speaking of these sects he states his belief that "the motive of the Manichean doctrines and of witchcraft is one and the same, and the punishment of the Manicheans and of witches was the same death at the stake. The fact that these heretics were recognized as sorcerers will explain, as nothing else can, the severity of the statutes against them, evidence of no ordinary depravity, and early in the eleventh century Manichee and warlock were regarded as synonymous." One must, indeed, see more than the merely logical identification of which Carus speaks, and thus far I may agree with Summers. But when he continues to expand the view that though "in some sense witchcraft was a descendant of the old pre-Christian magic . . . witchcraft as it existed in Europe from the eleventh century was mainly the spawn of the Gnostic heresy," and that "only a theologian can adequately treat of the subject," then I am unable to agree. Summers, in fact, shows us the readiness with which the Catholic Church would credit the witches and their god with the supernatural powers which they claimed. Thus, though he allows that the witch god was often a man in disguise, he makes the following statement: "But in many cases it is certain—and orthodoxy forbids us to doubt the possibility—that the Principle of Evil, incarnate, was present for the hideous adoration of his besotted worshippers. Such is the sense of the Fathers, such is the conclusion of the theologians who have dealt with these dark abominations. Metaphysically it is possible; historically it is indisputable." This point of view in 1926 may strike some readers as strange. Still, it will serve to explain the bitterness of the attack and the determination of the medieval Christians to fight this 'heresy' and the devil in person by any manner of means.

In the twelfth century the Church girded up its loins. The term 'Inquisitor,' for a judge in matters of faith, was first used in 1163; and in 1184 all relapsed 'heretics' were to be handed over to the secular authorities for capital punishment. Then Pope Innocent III., in order to crush the Albigenses in Provence, gave his emissaries power to sue all heretics, and, at the instigation of Castello Dominic and the Bishop of Toulouse, instituted the new order of the Dominicans. In the thirteenth century, the Albigenses were almost exterminated by his crusade against them; the Inquisition, or 'Holy Office,' was made a regular institution in 1229; and the Dominicans were appointed as papal inquisitors. The weight of this machinery for persecution and the weapon of the crusade were now felt throughout Europe. The Bastille was built in France because the prisons could no longer hold the vast numbers of suspected heretics who were awaiting trial. Germany was a most troubled area. Fisherfolk, for example, like our fishers and sailors to-day, are most prone to superstition, so we find Pope Gregory IX. preaching a crusade against the Stedingers of Friesland. He declared that they worshipped the devil under the name of Asmodi, and that the devil appeared to them in the form of a duck, a goose, or a youth, who, when they had kissed him and danced around him, would envelop them in total darkness, whereupon, they all, male and female, gave themselves up to debauchery. On May 27, 1234, the Crusaders are said to have killed 8,000 Stedingers. This was nothing to the horrors in Germany under the infamous emissary Conrad von Marburg, who was given such unlimited powers that no one was safe; and even the Archbishop of Mayence protested—in vain—against his iniquities. After his assassination Conrad was canonized as a saint and martyr. The same tale is told all over the West, and, though there were lulls when the Church was weak or during the great schism between Rome and Avignon, the persecutions became even more fiendish in the fifteenth century. Nider then published his appalling work *Formicarius de maleficiis*, and at the same time Pope Eugenius IV. urged the Inquisition to proceed with great severity, 'summarily, without ado, and without any judiciary form.'

In 1484 we have the famous Bull of Innocent VIII., and to give some idea of the power of the witch obsession I will quote, from Summers, part of what he refers to as "a truly noble and magnificent exordium." "It has indeed lately come to Our ears . . . that in some parts of North Germany . . . many persons of both sexes, unmindful of their own salvation and straying from the Catholic Faith, have abandoned themselves to devils, incubi and succubi, and by their incantations, spells, conjurations, and other accursed charms and crafts, enormities, and horrid offences, have slain infants yet in the mother's womb, as also the offspring of cattle, have blasted the produce of the earth, the grapes of the vine, the fruits of trees, nay, men and women, beasts of burthen, herd-beasts as well as animals of other kinds, vineyards, orchards, meadows, pasture-land, corn, wheat, and all other cereals; these wretches furthermore afflict and torment men and women, beasts of burthen, herd-beasts, as well as animals of other kinds, with terrible and piteous pains and sore diseases, both internal and external; they hinder men from performing the sexual act and women from conceiving, whence husbands cannot know their wives nor wives receive their husbands; over and above this they blasphemously renounce that Faith which is theirs . . ." This Bull was the immediate cause of the *Witch-hammer*, or *Malleus maleficarum*, by Sprenger and Kramer, which Carus rightly stigmatizes as "one of the most famous or infamous books ever written." Indeed, this work so ordered the procedure of a witch trial that the accused person had no possible chance of escape. Thus armed the campaign was carried out with great thoroughness. Untold numbers perished and thousands of victims, rather than endure the horrible torments applied by the agents of the Church, confessed to crimes which they had never committed. At Basle in 1474 even a cock was tried on the devilish charge of having laid an egg, and though its lawyer pleaded that there was no record of the devil ever having made a compact with one of the brute creation, and that, in any case, the laying of an egg was an involuntary act, and, as such, not punishable by law, his client was condemned to death and burned at the stake with due solemnity as a sorcerer in disguise.

This foolish, but true, tale illustrates the manner in which the human mind had become obsessed by the idea of the devil. And since the indigenous witch religion had become identified with devil worship, the more general conception found its specific outlet in an attack upon every person and everything that might possibly be connected with this cult. The medieval and the theological mind also recurred constantly to the savage belief that any form of illness (or even misfortune and death) which could not be readily attributed to natural causes was due to evil magic. This belief was, and can still be, a great obstacle to the progress of medicine and sanitation. It was clearly expressed in 1508 by the Abbot Trithemius in his *Antipalus Maleficiorum*. Having distinguished four classes of wizards and witches—viz., those who hurt or kill others by poison or natural methods; those who do so by magical arts; those who converse with the devil personally; and those who have actually made a contract with him—this learned divine concluded that the only method of dealing with these folk was to burn them alive. He says: " It is to be lamented that the number of witches in all countries is very great; for, indeed, there is not a village, be it ever so small, which does not harbour at least one of the third and of the fourth class. But how rare are the judges who punish these crimes against God and nature." As any savage might do, he laments the fact that " Men and animals die through the infamy of these women, and none considers that it is due to the malignity of witchcraft. There are many who suffer from serious diseases and do not even know that they are bewitched." However, during periods of unrest and when the priests thus enlarged their ignorance, the people were only too ready to persecute. It is only fair to say that the secular authorities were sometimes as zealous as the Inquisitors in the destruction of suspects and witch communities; and with more reason. The sect of the Albigenses, for example, offered a refuge to many criminals, runaway wives, and serfs, and, moreover, such sects, by denying the validity of the Christian oath, struck at the essential bond which bound together the whole fabric of the feudal system. False charges were also made for motives of private vengeance and despoliation; the innocent often suffered with the guilty. Lastly, these black centuries of relentless conflict left their mark both on the witch cult and the Catholic Church. The witch mania and mutual terror and hatred brought out the worst and most savage elements in the rival organizations.

The witch cult hunted and tortured by the 'hounds of God' became malignant. In many areas only fanatics and the most extreme types of perverted or ambitious men and women dared to incur the terrible penalties to which they were exposed. The Church also had long offered a rival field in which the born magician could employ his talents with greater honour and safety, and religious houses into which misfits from a social point of view could be safely thrust. Save in outlying lands and during brief periods of recrudescence the cult ceased to be a folk affair, rooted in the life of a community as a whole, and lost much of the joyous aspect of the folk festival or village rite. It became essentially a secret cult; the Sabbath was lost and only the Esbat remained, a meeting of sorcerers mainly given over to the black magic of hate. This is the usual form in which the witch organization is presented by the Catholic historian or theologian at the present day.

As far as the conflict was run on supernatural lines it is interesting to note that, in accordance with the usual procedure of imitative magic, each party would try to seize upon the rites of their opponents and turn them to their own advantage, both in defensive and in offensive warfare. To use a familiar phrase, a great deal of magic (like homeopathy) is based on the principle of taking the 'hair of the dog that bit you' as an antidote to the bite or as a protection against the aforesaid dog. Thus the witch, though it was not part of her specific ritual, was popularly supposed to reinforce her own incantations by repeating the Lord's Prayer backwards. Such methods were elaborated in the Black Mass when the witches would use consecrated wafers, that had been stolen, or make triangular black wafers of their own. By a further evolution little might be left of the old witch ritual, until we arrive at performances like the " Mass of S. Secaire," that must be conducted by a renegade priest whom only the Pope can shrive for this deadly sin. Such sophisticated rites, reinforced by alien streams and modern drugs, are still carried out by small coteries of perverts. According to Summers, " Satanists yet celebrate the Black Mass in London, Brighton, Paris, Lyons, Bruges, Berlin, Milan, and, alas! in Rome itself. . . . Often they seem to concentrate their vile energies in quiet cathedral cities of England, France, and Italy."

Conversely, the faith of the simpler Christians had to be strengthened against the real power, or, in other words, the overwhelming fear, of black magic, by the essential rites and symbols of the higher faith and others of a more dubious character, which Modernists justify by their theory of accommodation—*i.e.*, ' the toleration of harmless illusions of the day having little or no connection with religion.' If the witches worked magic by the use of the fat of an unbaptized child, dead men's bones, ' the hand of glory,' etc., the Church counteracted by a host of relics, or the torturers of Nuremberg drank a filthy decoction of witches' ashes as a prophylactic against their spells. Just as toxin working in an animal produces ' anti-bodies ' far in excess of the requirements of the beast, so by a similar process of hypertrophy, one may say that the venom of the witches produced an excessive number of anti-bodies in the medieval Church. I will not dilate upon the duplication of relics, for an old list will be found in *A very profitable Treatise, made by M. Jhon Calvyne,* and more recent exhibits confused Mark Twain; nor upon the swarm of unauthorized relic-mongers who were ready to show anything from a stone which had helped on the martyrdom of St. Stephen to a feather from the wing of the Holy Ghost. The fact remains that the Catholic Church became overloaded with practices and objects that were deemed ' superstitious ' largely as a result of its reaction against the medieval obsession of the devil in general and the witch god in particular.

After the Reformation the mania died down for awhile.

On the one hand, religion became less material in its outlook; and on the other, the Catholics and the Protestants became deeply engrossed in persecuting each other. But soon the witch-hunts began again in North Germany, Sweden, and the British Isles, where James I. favoured the world with his views on demonology, and the Calvinists came next to the Catholics in their cold-blooded cruelty and arrogance. We may, perhaps, see in Scotland and on our wilder moors the last stand of the cult as a hereditary belief, and as a reaction against the repression of various reformed beliefs, which allowed but few safety-valves for man's natural zest in life. Safety-valves like the Midlent Carnival, Twelfth Night, the reign of the Lords of Misrule (whose appointment by the Lord Mayor of London lasted from Allhallond Eve till Candlemas), and the old Saturnalia and Feasts of Janus, to which the Puritan Prynne in his *Histrio-Mastix* unkindly compares "our Bacchanalian Christmas and New Years' Tides."

A troubled environment would also lead to occasional revivals of some importance. "In the latter half of the eighteenth century the territory of Limburg was terrorized by a mysterious society known as 'The Goats.' These wretches met at night in a secret chapel, and after the most hideous orgies, which included the paying of divine honours to Satan and other foul blasphemies of the Sabbat, they donned masks fashioned to imitate goats' heads and sallied forth in bands to plunder and destroy. From 1772 to 1774 alone the tribunal of Foquemont condemned four hundred Goats to

the gallows. But the organization was not wholly exterminated until about the year 1780, after a régime of

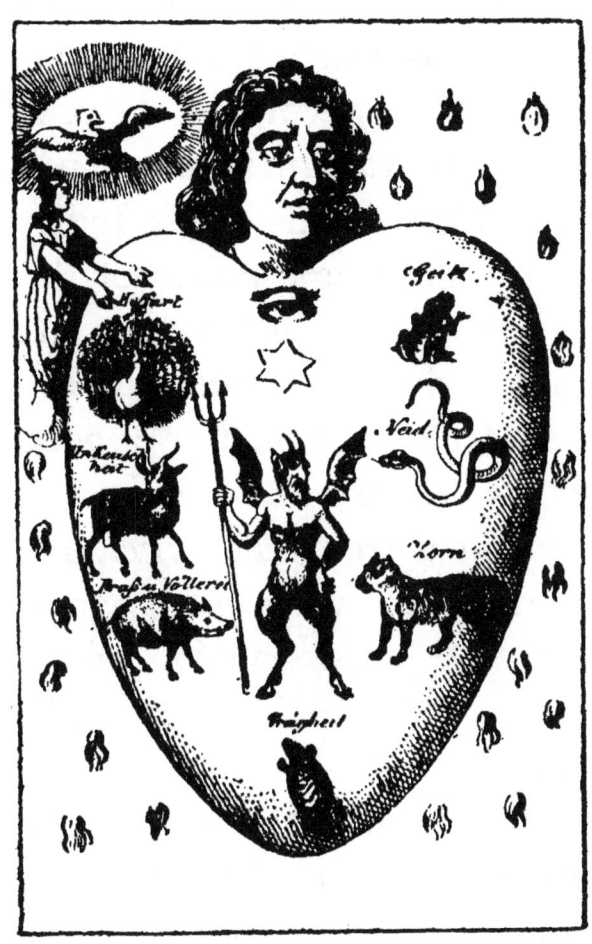

FIG. 5.—THE NATURAL STATE OF MAN.

A late representation of the traditional devil from "Das Herz des
Menschen" (1815), a reprint of an anonymous French work of the
eighteenth century. The peacock stands for pride; the toad for greed;
the goat for lust; the serpent for envy; the boar for gluttony; the lion
for anger; the tortoise for sloth. (From Carus' *History of the Devil.*
Open Court Publishing Co.)

the most repressive measures and unrelaxing vigilance"
(Summers). We have also the well-known outbreaks in
New England, which were partly a reaction against the

joyless and remarkably intolerant system of the Puritans and partly a response to a new wilderness that was full of danger and primeval fear. There were also settlers from East Anglia, which was ever a strong witch area; and has, indeed, witches not wholly white at the present day. This New England revival was burnt out, but a parallel development exists to-day in the West Indies as 'voodoo,' where we still have the magic power of the rabbit's paw, the sacrifice of the cock, and in Hayti as late as 1888 that of a human being, 'the Goat without Horns.' Much of this magic is of African origin, but 'voodoo' is derived from the Creole 'Vaudoux,' and this from 'Vaudois' and early French colonists from the witch area, where the stubborn Waldenses lived, whose seed would seem to have fallen on a black but most fruitful soil. Elsewhere, in civilized lands, the religion of the horned god seems to have disappeared in its pristine form. Slowly the misconception of much 'evil' passed in the seventeenth and the eighteenth centuries. Holland abolished witch persecution in 1610, Geneva in 1632, Sweden in 1649, England in 1682; while the last victims of the Inquisition, a Quaker and a Jew, were respectively hanged and burned in 1826. As ever with magic, it was knowledge rather than faith that brought about this change. The microscope and medical science, for example, had revealed the fact that many diseases are not necessarily the result of 'sin' or of demoniac possession; and that, let us say, quinine is a better protection than an amulet against malaria, and exorcism may be ineffective against a lesion in the brain.

Thus, magic that is pretentious and outworn will slowly disappear, and with it the power of the old magician in governance or in opposition. Some may, perhaps, hold that

FIG. 6.—SATAN'S RETURN WITH SEVEN OTHER SPIRITS MORE WICKED THAN HIMSELF.

Here evil has triumphed. In a companion picture in "Das Herz des Menschen" good has prevailed; and the devil and the seven vices are replaced by the symbols of Christianity. (From Carus' *History of the Devil.* Open Court Publishing Co.)

the horned god still can be found in the personal devil, and he, as Carus says, "is dead in science, but he is still alive even in Protestant countries among the number of

151

the uneducated, and the number of these is legion." He may, perhaps, be cherished as long as some men draw comfort from the belief that their opponents, if they do not suffer in this world, will do so in the next; and other men fear that the loss of a personal devil may imperil their belief in a personal god; that the loss of a definite shadow may detract from their vision of a being, made in their own image, by whom the shadow is cast. This possibility is beyond my theme, and I will conclude with some survivals, not of the central figure, but of his scattered rites.

CHAPTER IX

MAGIC TO-DAY

The case of the Abbé Desnoyers—The Giant of Cerne Abbas—Horseshoes and the sign of the horn—Pagan joy and Eastern doubt—
The dupe of God—Herlechin and harlequin—Mummers and
vagabonds—Witches' dances, old and new—The Horn Dance
summary—Reindeer once more.

THE end of the last chapter might well have been the end
of this book; and yet if these studies, or indeed any
studies of the past, are to have value, save as a diversion
or as an escape from the problems of our own times, they
must be related to the present. In other words, we must
recognize that the old impulses and beliefs and credulities
are still at work in the minds of living men; in minds
which are not greatly changed although their desires may
be expressed in a different form. Now and again I have
hinted at this; but I must leave each reader to interpret
these suggestions as best he may. So, in conclusion, I will
only take a few of the odd survivals in recent years.

If the last judicial execution for witchcraft in Europe
took place in Poland in 1793, when two old women were
burned at the stake, unlawful attempts upon the lives of
wizards and witches still continued. In our own country,
in 1865, a wizard was subjected to the ordeal by water at
Castle Headington, and though, according to this unfair

test, he proved his innocence by sinking to the bottom—a guilty person is supposed to swim—he died of shock on the following day. It was at the beginning of this century that two Irish peasants tried to roast a witch on her own fire. It was in January, 1926, that two men were summoned at Tipton, in Staffordshire, for threatening a van dweller who had, they declared, bewitched the wife of the one and the sister of the other; and some witnesses testified on oath that they were afraid to go near the woman because of her evil spells. But the best case comes from France, where a certain Abbé Desnoyers, priest of Bombon, near Melun, was seized and flogged for having bewitched a Madame Mesmin of Bordeaux. His assailants were arrested, and I append a bald statement, not from Nider's *Formicarius*, but from *The Times* of January 25, 1926. "The prisoners arrived at Melun. . . . The younger of the men, a street sweeper, aged 27, when confronted with the Abbé, had no hesitation in identifying him as Satan himself. The Abbé had, he said, sent diseases to Bordeaux from Bombon by means of birds, which flew over Mme. Mesmin's gardens, and their droppings gave rise to fungi of obscene shapes, which emitted such appalling odours that those who breathed them were smitten with horrible diseases. He himself had contracted a disease in this unusual fashion. Mme. Mesmin had a boil and her eyes were bloodshot. He added, unofficially, that the Abbé Desnoyers was one of the greatest sorcerers of the age. He was even more powerful that the Syrian Archimandrite, who had persecuted Mme. Mesmin six years ago. He could cause the death of anyone he liked in twenty-four hours, with or without suffering. A priest sold to the Devil was all-powerful. He had at his disposal dolls into which one stuck pins in order to injure one's enemies, and his were the spells which were transmitted by birds." Here, at least, there is one grain of reality, for I have no doubt that the fungi belonged to a not uncommon but most remarkable species, the 'Stinkhorn Fungus,' that so well deserves the name of *Ithyphallus impudicus*. I can testify to its smell, for a friend was about to have his drains up before we discovered a group of these fungi in his shrubbery. Its slimy spores, however, are not carried by birds, but by bluebottles and other carrion flies which the smell attracts; nor is the smell, so far as I know, likely to produce any disease, save one of the imagination.

Of the activities of certain coteries that are called Satanists I can say little, but their rites appear to be of an eclectic rather than an indigenous nature. In the East native cults may exist; but in the West the result of the persecution was to stamp out the central fires so that only a few sparks of operative witchcraft still smoulder here and there. Even in Britain, late in the last century, spells for death or love (since the melting of wax can also be interpreted as melting the heart of an obdurate lover) were being wrought with waxen images, effigies of clay or straw, a beast's heart, or a toad stuck full of pins or thorns, and an arrangement, well-known in Italy, made by knotting the feathers of a black hen into a cord, was found in an English belfry in 1886 and was recognized by an old villager as a 'witches' ladder.' We may again recall the Gallizenæ when Sir John Rhys tells us " that the faculty of turning oneself into a hare at will is regarded as hereditary in certain families in Wales "; and that, though in the case of his nurse who belonged to such a family, the matter was treated as a joke, he had himself been warned not to question the inhabitants of a valley near Snowdon about witch hares.

Or, again, we may look to that stark figure at Cerne Abbas. " There are," writes W. H. Hudson in 1903, " many old legends about Cerne—that St. Augustine came here, for instance, and caused the water forming St. Austin's Well, a clear spring just by the abbey, to flow; also that the natives, who were pagans, mocked him and his monks and drove them forth, and as a mark of contempt pelted them with fishes' tails, which stuck to their robes. The saint prayed that God would send some sign to turn these peoples' hearts, and the sign sent was that all the children thereafter were born with tails—fish tails, but some say cow tails. It is a belief in Cerne to this day that the lineal descendants of the people who mocked the saint are still born with tails. It is also believed that to ensure that a child shall be healthy and strong it should be taken soon after birth and bathed in St. Austin's Well —the spring where the people get their drinking water; and that the dipping should take place just when the sun-beams touch the water. About the figure of the Giant, too, there are some old beliefs, one being that a childless woman can be cured of her barrenness by sitting on the figure. But others maintain that to ensure fertility, the marriage must be consummated on the figure." Here we have the explanatory legend to account for tailed men, and, though Hudson speaks of marriage, a rite which was in reality an ante-nuptial practice, like the 'island custom' at Portland and similar customs that are common elsewhere, and may or may not be associated with some special place. So, also, there are many other charms and spells that anyone may discover if he truly knows the folk—and does not stay at the vicarage.

Again, if fear of this cult has left its mark upon the Catholic Church, it has also left many curious beliefs in the common mind of the people. Horseshoes, the old protection against the witch, are nailed above doors and windows in any village. Many object to the coven number of thirteen, which one of our railways has just abolished on sleeping cars. We do not deal our cards or pass the wine against the sun, otherwise widdershins, as the witches danced. Over the greater part of the West it is not tactful to make the sign of the horned hand, and it is impolite, as it was in Falstaff's day, to connect antlers with a married man. The widespread use of the horns, be they in the form of a horseshoe, a coral ornament like those of Italy, or a sign manual, testifies to its antiquity and demands an explanation. Thus Rèmy de Gourmont remarks that, " in the deer family, with the exception of the reindeer, the males alone have horns, and this is the origin, by no means an absurd one, of a very old pleasantry, since the does are also very lascivious and willingly welcome many males." Such biological origins are, of course, common: we find them in our plebeian use of such words as 'goat,' 'ram,' 'bitch,' and many more; and in the derivation of 'cuckold' from cuckoo, that most wanton and polyandrous of all birds. I cannot, however, help connecting the sign of the horns with the cult of the witch god and the old magician. Once that gesture may well have conveyed to a husband the suggestion that his wife had taken part in the Sabbath rites, or the suspicion that she would like to do so. It is the common, unkindly use of the sign, like a string dangled before a man whose brother has been hung. Less obviously the use of the horned hand as a protection against the 'evil eye' may be one of the frequent instances in which the magic of one's opponent is employed as a defensive measure. Nor need the value of such a sign have been psychological alone; if it had ever been the password or secret signal amongst initiates. So, also, we may still find the broom, once the magic wand or bâton and the witch's steed, placed across the threshold—successfully so I was once told by an old villager—to prevent the witch from entering the house. In a final degeneration I can only look to the broom as the most likely source of many superstitions that have now become attached to that most modern and homely article, the umbrella. The horseshoe I cannot account for, unless we can see the same horn symbolism; but cold iron was ever a sovereign spell against the magic of an older race that had only bronze or stone; and in faith as well as fact a smith, like St. Dunstan, was often called upon not only to forge swords against the aborigines, but to cast out the ancient gods. The current superstitions concerning salt, not to mention its use in holy water, may also have some connection with the fact that salt is said never to have been used in the witch ceremonies. But the beliefs that have survived from ancient creeds are so abundant and so attenuate that the list would be endless and their definite derivation would be most difficult. None the less, some attention might be paid to the prejudice against red in certain connections; the Easter rabbit or hare and other animals; parsley and other plant superstitions; and many death portents in an animal form. Most of these, however, are concerned with fear, with the abominable aspect of the magician, and I would end on a more cheerful note.

For, if the witch cult in its later phase degenerated into a creed of hate, as any religion may under persecution or when baser minds seek to exploit their fellow-men by fear, it once had some elements of joy and ecstasy. This point is denied by theologians, who, though they speak of pagan joy, prefer to regard this cult as heresy, and by inquisitors, who wish to justify their deeds. But even in their accounts, fear, joy, and the envy of the celibate may be most strangely mixed.

Summers thus transcribes from Spinosa's *Tractatus de Strigis et Lamiis* (Venice, 1533) an account given by a peasant who stumbled upon the Sabbath while he was crossing a waste at three in the morning in the district of Mirandola: " In the distance he suddenly caught sight of what seemed to be numerous fires flitting to and fro, and as he drew nearer he saw that these were none other than large lanthorns held by a bevy of persons who were moving here and there in the mazes of a fantastic dance, whilst others, as at a rustic picnic, were seated partaking of dainties and drinking stoups of wine, what time a harsh music, like the scream of a cornemuse, droned through the air. Curiously no word was spoken, the company whirled and pirouetted, ate and drank, in strange and significant silence. Perceiving that many, unabashed, were giving themselves up to the wildest debauchery and publicly performing the sexual act with every circumstance of indecency, the horrified onlooker realized that he was witnessing the revels of the Sabbat. Crossing himself fervently and uttering a prayer he drove as fast as possible from the accursed spot, not, however, before he had recognized some of the company as notorious evil-doers and persons living in the vicinity who were already under the grave suspicion of sorcery." We have similar accounts from Spain, France, and Scotland, in which special mention is made of tables spread with wine and delicate (also indelicate) meats and of lively dances accompanied by the music of violins, flutes, citterns, hautboys, tambourines, and the bagpipes, and so intricate that when some Italian children showed them to the Inquisitors "it was evident that they had been instructed by no mere human tutelage" (Summers).

One might, indeed, on most general lines be tempted to see in the contest between the old religion and the new a conflict between a primitive, unabashed, and very natural delight in the pleasures of the flesh and the material beauty of this world on the one hand, and on the other that unnatural, monkish, and Eastern asceticism which will ruin a body to save a soul and will damn this world and most of its inhabitants to enhance the value of some future paradise for the elect. But such a distinction, though it has been made, would be as partial as the later idealization of the witches as good fairies. They were merely women. And so I will leave any such false and invidious distinctions to take up two threads of devolution which still survive.

Where men fear they are apt to use ridicule as a means of defence; and, when the witch cult became more hostile and more alienated from the realities of life, the more civilized people began to ridicule the devil in his aboriginal form. There are countless legends in which the witch god or devil appears as a trusting fool and is outwitted by the shallowest forms of trickery and saintly dishonesty. Our stage is liturgical in origin, and we can see this attitude in our early plays, where " the Devil appeared in spite of his smartness as the dupe of God; his fate was always to be defeated and ridiculed. As such he figures in the mysteries, the Easter and Christmas plays, in which he acts one of the important parts, that of intriguer, harlequin, and fool." I have quoted Carus owing to his mention of harlequin, though he does not seem to be aware of harlequin's past history. Summers also notes that as late as the fifteenth century " The devil was represented as black, with goat's horns, ass's ears, cloven hoofs, and an immense phallus. He is, in fact, the Satyr of the old Dionysiac processions, a nature-spirit, the essence of joyous freedom and unrestrained delight, shameless if you will, for the old Greeks knew not shame. He is the figure who danced light-heartedly across the Aristophanic stage, stark nude in broad midday, animally physical, exuberant, ecstatic, crying aloud the primitive refrain, 'Phales, boon mate of Bacchus, joyous comrade in the dance, wanton wanderer o' nights' . . . in a word, he was Paganism incarnate, and Paganism was the Christian's deadliest foe; so they took him, the Bacchic reveller, they smutted him from horn to hoof, and he remained the Christian's deadliest foe, the Devil." This black, phallic figure with goat horns and a tail could still be found on the cover of *A Courtly Masque: The Device called, The World tos't at Tennis*, in 1620; and here we may recognize the form of the old magician more readily than a more abstract conception of the Evil One (Plate VII.). This method of presentation gave way to such forms as Mephistopheles; just as the hunter who sells his soul gave way to the " Flying Dutchman " and Faust; and at the same time the poets produced their Pucks and Fairy Queens, who were merely uncertain, freakish, and mischievous.

In 1685 we have William Mountfort's play, *The Life and Death of Doctor Faustus. Made into a farce, with the Humours of Harlequin and Scaramouch*, in which the first spangled harlequin appeared on the English stage. From this I will hark back to herlechin, for if in England herlechin had become lost in the wild hunter or smothered by the stage devil, in Italy Dante's demon 'alichino' had, by a like process of ridicule, become 'Arlechino,' a familiar figure in early comedy. This character was for awhile modelled upon that of a Bergamasque serving-man, who indulged in many silly-shrewd quips which were supposed to be native to the town of Bergamo. In the sixteenth century this character passed into France, Spain, and England still as a wit and jester; but then he met another tradition and became silent. He became that mysterious flitting, dancing figure, clad in his parti-coloured dress, a hat or mask which by a stage fiction makes him invisible, and bearing his magic wand. In the mask the writer of the *Quarterly Review* sees the vestige of Odin's 'tarn-kappe,' the Saxon 'heoloth-helm,' the 'cap of darkness,' the *petasus* worn alike and for similar reasons by Hermes, by Charon, and by Aita, the Pluto of the Etruscans. The lathe, by which harlequin transforms the street scene of the pantomime into a fairyland, he sees as Odin's magic staff; and in the chequered garb he sees the 'flecked coat of Odin,' and many tempest gods, and a wind symbolism in the whirling dance. Such symbolic meanings may have been added to the central figure, and Harlequin's play with Columbine has been related to the poetic myth of Pluto and Persephone; but long before myth I prefer to see the simpler god of the underworld, the whirling dance of the wizard, even the bâton and mask and the striped legs of the old magician; the spear, the war-paint, the camouflage of the ancient hunter.

More might be added concerning the witch cult and the

stage. The denunciations of the Puritans and other kill-joys were probably heightened by the presence of such a connection in the mind of man; as well as the pleasure that men derived from the old mystery plays, and the regrettable fact that the stage often presents our 'vile flesh,' 'this vale of tears,' and even human love in an attractive form. One could cite the old laws which class together actors, rogues, and vagabonds; and in France, I am informed, deny an actor the right to a Christian burial. One could also recall many queer superstitions that are still current, like the black cat placed on the first-night stage of a London theatre to secure good luck. Truly the magician should have priority as the patron saint of mummers.

And there is more beside, for we shall never know, though we may well suspect, our debt to the old religion for many a dance, for ballads (*ballata*) set to a dancing tune, for ribald songs that blast the pretentious pessimist, for joyous music that truly thrills our hearts. La Volta, a witch dance, is said to be the origin of the valse. The Tarentelle, if not a witch dance, was a survival from a Dianic or Dionysiac cult, whose celebrants, to disguise their real activities, circulated the strange tale that their ecstatic frenzy was caused by a spider's bite. Even as I write, a dance now known as the Charleston has become popular, with a peculiar step that is said to be derived from voodoo ritual; while similar importations such as the "Bunny Hug" and "Black Bottom" may be interpreted in a like manner. The strange attraction of such novelties

PLATE VIII

THE HORN DANCE AT ABBOTS BROMLEY.

General view of the dancers. Front row, left to right:—a deer; the fool, or leader, with a jester's cap and wand; the sportsman with his bow; a deer; the hobbyhorse and its rider with a whip. Back row:—the remaining deer; Maid Marian, wearing a gown and a moustache; the musician with a bowler hat and a concertina. (Reproduced by permission from the Sir Benjamin Stone Collection of photographs in the Birmingham Reference Library.)

lies in their antiquity and in their genuine appeal to the natural emotions of mankind; or the less natural desires of the magician's crew in decadence.

But by way of a conclusion let me turn to indigenous growths and the folk dances of the British Isles. There are the Northern sword-dances which culminate in the death, or in the death and the resurrection, of one of the characters; and similar childish games which have a Viking or Nordic tone. But in the Grenoside dance the captain is partly animalized by wearing a rabbit's skin upon his helm, and the 'Betty' at Earsdon was formerly hung in a hairy cap. So, also, on Plough Monday—the origin of which, as antiquarians are wont to observe, 'dates back to pre-Reformation times'—a plough was drawn round the parish attended by a 'Bessy' and a 'Fool' clad in the skins of animals and having long tails. The sacramental feast on the flesh of the sacred animal was preserved in the Whit Hunt near the Forest of Wychwood, where three deer were killed and distributed for luck; at Hallaton where a 'hare-pie' feast brought luck; and in the lamb-pie feast at Kirtlington. Such examples might be multiplied, but I will content myself with the Horn Dance at Abbot's Bromley, which is held annually on Monday in Wakes Week, that is on the day following the first Sunday after the fourth of September (Plate VIII.). We can take the account given by Dr. Plot in his *Natural History of Staffordshire* (1686): "At Abbot's, or now rather Paget's Bromley, they had also, within memory, a sort of sport, which they celebrated at Christmas (on New Year and

Twelft-day) called the Hobby-horse dance, from a person that carried the image of a horse between his legs, made of thin boards, and in his hand a bow and arrow, which passing thro' a hole in the bow, and stopping upon a sholder it had in it, he made a snapping noise as he drew it to and fro, keeping time with the Music : with this man danced six others, carrying on their shoulders as many Rain deers heads, 3 of them painted white, and 3 red, with the armes of the cheif families (viz of Paget, Bagot, and Wells) to whom the revenews of the town cheifly belonged, depicted on the palms of them, with which they danced the Hays, and other Country dances. To this Hobby-horse dance there also belong'd a pot, which was kept by turnes, by 4 or 5 of the cheif of the Town, whom they call'd Reeves, who provided Cakes and Ale to put in this pot; all people who had any kindness for the good intent of the Institution of the sport, giving pence a piece for themselves and families; and so forragners too, that came to see it : with which Mony (the charge of the Cakes and Ale being defrayed) they not only repaired their Church but kept their poore too : which charges are not now perhaps so cheerfully born." To this we will add Cecil Sharp's account of the dance as he found it at the present day. The music of the dance is not traditional, nor need the complicated movements detain us, but the characters will. These seem to vary slightly, according to the local talent that is available. Sharp speaks of the 'deer' or the six dancers with the horns; then 'Maid Marion,' a man disguised as a woman carrying a ladle for the collection;

the man with the Hobby-horse, the jaw of which snaps in time with the music; the 'Boy' also clicking his bow and arrow; and the 'Fool,' with his cap and bells, bearing a stick and bladder or a lathe to enliven the proceedings. Plot does not mention Maid Marion or the Fool, but both a fool or a leader and a female impersonation, more usually known as the 'Bess,' are original constituents of similar dances and mumming plays elsewhere. In the account that accompanies the photographs taken by Sir Benjamin Stone in 1899, the Hobby-horse rider is called 'Robin Hood' and the Boy is spoken of as the 'Sportsman'; and it describes how " the 'deer' step to a lively tune, the sportsman making believe to shoot them and letting off his bow and arrow with a 'clack' in time with the music; and now and again Robin Hood slashes them with his whip to keep them moving." The names of Robin Hood and Maid Marion do not matter since the names of local or popular celebrities so often become attached to primitive characters, as is the case with Drake upon Dartmoor, or, as a true and excellent example, a Berkshire farmer's wife informed a friend of mine that in a recent trip to the Highlands she had been most interested in " the cave where Sir Walter Scott had watched the spider while he was hiding from Oliver Cromwell."

But under these changing forms what a wonderful blend and summary of tradition one may see, if one cares to view this dance by the light of a magic candle. Then the Fool stands out as the chief devil, who, though the name hints at the devil's decline as a lord of misrule or the mumming

167

jester with ass's ears instead of horns, none the less appears in the photographs as the oldest, most dignified, and most responsible member of the troop. Nor is the second devil lacking with the whip, now placed in the hands of the horseman. Lastly, in Maid Marion, or 'Moll,' we might see the 'Reine du Sabat,' or even that vaguer Dianic queen of Elphin.

And behind this lies the still older symbolism, the oldest play in the world, of men disguised as wild food animals which in mimetic magic the hunter, with his bow and arrow, pretends to slay. One would, indeed, like to know the history of these horns, but my inquiries have failed. What is stranger still, according to some zoologists, they are not the horns of the European reindeer, but fine trophies (they weigh about eighty to ninety pounds the pair) of the caribou or American reindeer. The two species are closely allied, but if this identification is correct, they must have been brought back from the New World by some early hunter whose name and tale have been alike forgotten. And yet they carry us, if only by a remarkable coincidence, back to that cult of the Reindeer Men over which the magician ruled.

INDEX

INDEX

INDEX

INDEX

CPSIA information can be obtained
at www.ICGtesting.com
Printed in the USA
LVHW101530280120
645067LV00004B/377

9 781162 605722